SO-AXJ-422

Priceless Gifts

Priceless Gifts

How to Give the Best to Those You Love

DANIEL A. SUGARMAN, PH.D.

BARNES
&NOBLE
BOOKS
NEW YORK

To Barbara
who gives these gifts to me

Copyright © 1978 by Daniel A. Sugarman

This edition published by Barnes & Noble, Inc.,
by arrangement with Curtis Brown, Ltd.

All rights reserved. No part of this book may be used or reproduced
in any manner whatsoever without the written permission of the Publisher.

2003 Barnes & Noble Books

ISBN 0-7607-4129-8

Printed and bound in the United States of America

03 04 05 06 M 9 8 7 6 5 4 3 2 1

FG

Contents

Contents

Preface

PRICELESS GIFTS was first published two decades ago. Although some of its details are out of date, its message about the gifts that bring true happiness and growth to the giver not only does not date, but is more pertinent today than ever before.

The last decade of the twentieth century became the climax of a psychological revolution that went awry. What began in the 1950s and 1960s as a healthy movement toward self-awareness and self-fulfillment grew into a frenzied search for immediate gratification and easy success. Pension plan rip-offs, phony bookkeeping practices, and a frantic search for the "dot.com buck" were in style. Drugs, vicious divorces, and ugly custody battles for children or property were in vogue. The psychological revolution that promised to lead its followers to eternal gratification instead took its new pleasure-seeking disciples into a life that promised psychological and personal disaster.

The events of September 11, 2001, and the exposé of the excesses of the 1990s, have resulted in a growing dissatisfaction with the current emphasis on material gifts. Many individuals have begun a soul-searching quest for meaning and have realized that true happiness often comes from giving themselves to others. *Priceless Gifts* is a helpful guide for people who want to have the tools to put into action their now growing conviction that *the best things in life aren't things!*

Daniel A. Sugarman, Ph.D.
January 2003

Introduction

It wasn't very long ago that psychologists began to find that the reason some people were unhappy and depressed was because they always put their own needs last. After a while, some got so far out of touch with their own feelings and desires that they no longer knew what they were feeling or even what they wanted.

We found that it is important for people to get in touch with their feelings, and healthy for them to know who they are, to become more self-accepting, to express their feelings, to take responsibility for their actions, and to continue to learn and to grow.

Taking care of our own needs can help us grow; but the line between "enough" and "too much" is a narrow one, since taking care of our own needs *at the expense of the needs of others* can make us shrink. Consequently, many people who have already become their own best friends must now learn to find joy in befriending others.

We are given a good example of what this means in the story, now more than two thousand years old, of a man who was planting a carob tree. A passerby asked him why he was taking the time and effort to plant the tree, since the fruit would take seventy years to mature. The man replied, "I found the world provided with carob trees because my ancestors planted them for me. I am planting them now for my children."

The passerby's reply was not recorded, so we have no way of knowing what he said. But if this incident happened in our day and age, his response might very well be:

"What a damn-fool thing to do! Why don't you take care of yourself? You should make some jewelry out of those carob seeds so you'll look super when you go out. The kids can worry about themselves, and if they aren't happy about it when they grow up, they can always see a psychologist! They're too spoiled as it is."

Priceless Gifts challenges this "me-first" philosophy. The book is about people and self-help, psychology, and growing up. But most of all, it's about the important things that you can give to those you love.

Priceless Gifts

I. The Joy of Giving

Behold, I do not give lectures or a little charity,
When I give, I give myself.

—WALT WHITMAN, *Leaves of Grass*

DURING THE FIRST YEARS of our lives, we are completely concerned with ourselves and with self-gratification.

A little later on, we begin to conform to the rules of the group, not because we agree with them, but because we yield to social pressure. If we continue to grow, we reach an even higher level of development in which we delight in giving. At this stage, most of us like to give more than we like to take. We want to leave the world a better place than when we found it. We care! We give! Such people enjoy planting carob trees.

Some people never grow; they remain takers and not givers. They are mostly in love with themselves. They are very much like Narcissus.

According to Greek mythology, Narcissus was a youth who caused the death of Echo by spurning her love. Narcissus could love only himself. Attempts to involve him in a relationship with other people would inevitably be thwarted by his excessive self-concern.

Narcissus was almost the direct opposite of the kind of person our ancient Judeo-Christian teachings tell us we should be. These traditions teach us that we should be giving, loving, and caring —and that great pleasure can be found in bringing joy to others.

Psychologists and psychiatrists have come to use the term *narcissistic* for those people who are entirely wrapped up in themselves.

A healthy person *must* be concerned with his or her own needs! But one *also* has to be concerned with the needs of others. The trick is to find a good balance. It's not always easy to do so.

Some psychologists feel that narcissistic people cannot give to others because they are simply too frightened and angry. By refusing to give, they sometimes frustrate others. It's a little like the old joke of the sadist and the masochist who took a walk together. According to this story, the masochist asks the sadist, "Please hit me!" The sadist replies with a wry smile, "No! I won't do that for you."

These days, almost everyone knows how important it is to take care of one's own needs and desires.

So what's new?

What's new is that many people are so busy taking such good care of their own needs that they hardly have *anything left over for anyone else!*

What's new is that this kind of behavior has very recently come to be regarded as chic and in and smart!

What's new is that plain, old-fashioned selfishness is too frequently now being called self-actualization.

What's new is that an awesome number of people are taking workshops in assertiveness training, when most of them would be far better off if they took a course in plain, old-fashioned manners!

Yes! Among many who should know better, taking is *in* and giving is *out*.

During the past few years, narcissism is in, and the carob-seed planter is out.

To be giving and concerned and committed to the needs of others is regarded, at best, as being quaint.

More often it's seen as being downright stupid.

After all, you don't want to be a sucker do you?

There were probably a great many things that happened in our society that created small streams of mistrust and self-interest. Soon these streams converged into a muddy river of cynicism.

During the past fifteen years, one of our presidents was killed on a sunny afternoon in Dallas. Another president resigned after he was found to have repeatedly lied.

Thousands of Americans were maimed or killed in a war that few supported. The crime rate continued to climb as the value of the dollar began to fall.

The old values of concern for others didn't seem to work anymore. Nothing seemed to work anymore. Nothing at all. Nothing!

Nothing ever lasts very long. Something comes to fill the void.

What came to fill the void created by the cynicism and disappointment was a new and overriding concern with one's own pleasure and needs!

Up with me! Down with you! (Unless, of course, you can help me achieve *my* needs and desires.)

Initially, the "me-firsters" felt a little guilty. After all, for years they had been taught that it was good to love one's neighbor as much as one's self. So lots of books and speakers and articles were needed to convince them that self-interest was the most important thing and that concern with the needs of others was archaic.

Ayn Rand's *The Virtue of Selfishness* preached the message that the achievement of happiness was the individual's highest moral purpose.

A few years later, a little book about a seagull who could fly higher and better and more joyously than all the other seagulls became a national best seller. Jonathan Livingston Seagull was quite a bird! He wasn't too interested in the welfare of other birds. He didn't care much about the pollution of the waters or about the rapid overfishing of herring that could cause disaster for generations of seagulls yet to come. No! Jonathan Livingston Seagull was mostly interested in flying the highest and, of course, while doing so, having fun.

Lots of folks who were also having fun and flying high (with or without the use of drugs) felt that this special, fun-loving seagull was an important symbol for them.

Some even bought little gold or silver seagulls to hang around the neck. After all, one needed something to replace the discarded Cross or Star of David that used to hang there!

If Narcissus could have pulled himself away from his reflecting pool long enough, he could have cashed in on a good thing. He could have sold lots of attractive necklaces with his picture on it to those who were becoming converted to the joys of the New Religion of Narcissism.

The historian Will Durant wrote that "religions may come and go, but the need to believe is eternal."

Most often, when people profess certain religious beliefs, they *consciously* join that particular group. New Narcissism, however, gathers most of its members from the ranks of disillusioned dropouts. Most people who join New Narcissism don't even know that they belong! They join New Narcissism (hereafter referred to as NN) in an attempt to find happiness in a life that doesn't seem to be working for them. Some have never even heard of Narcissus. *All* are looking for pleasure and self-justification.

Any new religion needs prayers, customs, rules, rituals, high priests, and holy writings. NN has them *all!* Yes, indeed— there's nothing modest about NN.

1. There is a "prayer" by Fritz Perls that has become very popular with NN. "I do my thing, and you do your thing. I am not in this world to live up to your expectations. You are not in this world to live up to mine. I am I, and you are you. And if by chance we find each other, it's beautiful. If not, it can't be helped."

In *The Do-It-Yourself Psychotherapy Book,* Dr. Martin Shepard, a psychiatrist, advises the following use of the prayer: "Copy the following Gestalt Prayer. Place it on the bathroom mirror. Read it each morning and evening at tooth-brushing time."

2. Let's look at some of the basic "commandments" of NN.

   1. There shall be no one more important than you.
   2. You shall always act in your own best interest.
   3. You shall not let the interests of others interfere with your pleasure.
   4. If it's in your best interests to twist the truth, by all means do so.
   5. Don't expose children in school to basic skills. To do so could cause them to commit the worst sin of all—they could become *bored.*
   6. Don't have much to do with old folks. Old people can get forgetful or sick, and that would be very unpleasant.
   7. Nothing you do is *ever* wrong unless you get caught.
   8. You should not get involved in any group that is involved in social action (unless it will help you get elected to the school board).
   9. You should tell people what they want to hear—and then do what you want. You don't need a hassle.
   10. You are not subject to the same rules as everyone else.

3. Let's explore together some of the writings of NN. To illustrate how far we have progressed, I will contrast some of this profound new "wisdom" with some of the "old rubbish" that NN tries to clear out of the attics of your mind.

OLD RUBBISH?

"Always do right. This will gratify some people and astonish the rest."

—MARK TWAIN

NEW WISDOM?

"Now you know that being right truly doesn't matter—winning your game is what counts."

—CARL FREDERICK
EST: Playing the Game the New Way

"Conscience is the guardian in the individual of the rules which the community has evolved."

—SOMERSET MAUGHAM

"Clear your mind, then.... Forget the 'moral' standards that others may have tried to cram down your throat, forget the beliefs people may have tried to intimidate you into accepting as right...."

—ROBERT RINGER
Looking Out for Number 1

"It is not up to you to complete the work, yet you are not free to abstain from it."

—THE TALMUD

"Concentrate on looking out for Number One. I'm sure you have enough problems of your own without worrying about helping others...."

—ROBERT RINGER
Looking Out for Number 1

"So whatever you wish that men should do to you, do so to them; for this is the law...."

—MATTHEW 7:12
The Sermon on the Mount

"The foolish rules, traditions, and policies will never go away, but you don't have to be a part of them. Just shrug as others go through their sheep motions.... You'll find scores of everyday

7

occurrences where it is easier to
circumvent the rules quietly than
to start a protest movement."
—Dr. Wayne W. Dyer
Your Erroneous Zones

4. Let's look at some of the rituals of NN. If you have only a couple of weekends to spare, you can invest three hundred dollars and go to est (Erhard Seminar Training). This group, with headquarters in San Francisco, was founded by Werner Erhard.

   During most of the first weekend, you'll be inducted into this group by a skilled trainer who will use some not-so-choice language to describe you. If you're uncertain about parting with three hundred bucks to learn what part of the anatomy you resemble, you might be given a free pamphlet that tells you that, "Rats and human beings have one essential difference. Rats know only from cheese; humans want to be in the 'right' tunnel. . . ."

   If you have more time to spare, you might want to check into Esalen or any other "growth" center. The Esalen Institute, which uses encounter groups, is located in Big Sur, California. There, for a couple of weeks you can bathe nude in hot sulphur springs and make it with anyone who wants to make it with you.

   I don't know if the massages are included in the daily rate or if they take credit cards.

5. Who are some of the high priests of NN? As a psychologist, I have a confession to make. Many of the new high priests of NN are psychologists or psychiatrists who found it tough to think through some of the more difficult problems of human behavior. With a lotus leaf in one

hand and an electric vibrator in the other, some of these psychologists spend their time preaching the joys of the new hedonism.

In a recent article in the *American Psychologist,* Dr. George Albee expressed dismay at the pervasiveness in the many graduate training programs of the increased emphasis on feeling at the expense of thinking.

"Many of the new graduate humanistic therapy programs," Dr. Albee wrote, "have their resident guru or gurus who argue that learning to feel is far more important than learning to think, and that teaching students to be therapists and encounter-group manipulators does not require, indeed, may be inhibited by, a library. . . ."

Not unexpectedly, all is not joyous in NN!

CASE #1

Charles and Betty Phelps,* both age thirty, are having trouble with their son, Jeff, who is a year old. Jeff is teething and wakes up at night crying. Betty has to play tennis early in the morning, and she can't play well if she loses sleep. She calls her doctor to ask for a prescription to help Jeff sleep. Her doctor tells her that he doesn't want to prescribe anything. Betty changes pediatricians.

CASE #2

Richard Sandson, age forty, is annoyed at his wife, Judy. Richard has started an affair with a young woman whom he met at a recent convention. He feels that Judy has gained too much weight and that she gets too uptight when he tells her he wants to continue his new relationship.

---

* To protect the privacy of my patients, all such names in this book are fictitious.

CASE #3

Amy Ross, age fourteen, goes to her guidance counselor. She wants to drop out of her European History class. She explains that her class is not relevant. She obtains a transfer to a mini-course entitled "Dracula, Frankenstein, and the Occult."

CASE #4

Dr. Fred Kovak, age thirty-five, is a well-known psychologist. He doesn't see anything wrong in smoking pot even though it's illegal. He asks a young patient of his if he can bring him half a kilo of grass the next time the patient comes for a session.

CASE #5

Joyce Nodine, age twenty-eight, finds that she has become attracted to her next-door neighbor, Carl. He's taller than her husband, and he lasts longer in bed. Her husband comes home one day to an empty house, no children, and a Dear John letter. She finally contacts her husband to inform him that if he contests the divorce proceedings she will do her best to insure that he never sees the children.

❧

Giving is not as easy as it first seems. Even if we want to give a gift, we have to pick the right gift for the right person at the right time.

Many years ago, an Englishwoman, Lady Pamela Wyndham Glenconner, wrote:

Giving presents is a talent; to know what a person wants, to know when and how to get it, to give it lovingly, and well. Unless a character possesses this talent, there is no moment more annihilating to ease than that in which a present is received and given.

Sometimes a gift is not really a token of love but rather an expression of pure self-interest. People who fish don't give free worms to the fish without the expectation of some good return! Yes, many gifts have psychological hooks hidden somewhere.

There used to be a tribe of Indians who lived in the Pacific Northwest. These Indians would ruin their enemies by giving them gifts that would, of course, later have to be returned with interest. If Joe Indian were mad at Mike Indian, for example, he would invite Mike and the rest of his clan to a "giving"- ceremony that was called a potlatch.

At the potlatch Joe might give Mike a new canoe, lots of warm blankets, and the latest in fishing spears. All the while, there would be lots of speeches and plenty of good food. The hidden purpose of the potlatch was to embarrass Mike, who would be feverishly thinking about where he could ever find the resources to return such lavish gifts. And so the game of "Can You Top This?" would enter another round. Although hardly anyone gives potlatches anymore, I must confess I recently attended a couple of weddings that seemed suspicious.

Many people give gifts for the wrong reasons. Here are a few that are at the top of my "bad-gift" list.

1. The Guilt Gift
There's a dentist I know who has a hard job keeping away from the ladies. Everytime he gets involved in another affair, he begins to send his wife large bouquets of flowers. She would rather have loyalty than a dozen red roses!

2. The Gift That the Giver Really Wants
A young father bought his three-year-old son an elaborate set

of electric trains. The boy couldn't manage the trains and kept getting small electric shocks. He would rather have the box the trains came in!

3. The Gift That Is Really a Bribe
Several years ago a young surgeon joined the staff of a hospital. Shortly after he opened his office, he sent elaborate Christmas gifts to many of the general practitioners on the staff. They would rather have competence than another bottle of bourbon!

4. The Gift That Shows How Powerful We Are
One father, when his son turned seventeen and was able to get a driver's license, gave him a new Mercedes-Benz. Left with a feeling of inadequacy because of his own childhood encounter with poverty, this father needed to give his son not transportation, but a status symbol. The boy would have preferred a car that didn't cause catcalls in the parking lot of the local high school!

5. The Hate Gift
One woman I know is married to a man who has severe diabetes and has been placed on a very restricted diet. Sometimes, at a big party, she brings her husband a piece of cake or a particularly good cookie. "This won't hurt you, dear" are her words. Her actions, however, are calculated to make her husband sick. He would be better off with a plain glass of water—and a wife who liked him better! When it comes to gifts, it's not always easy to tell what's going on without a score card.

It's a little like the story of the psychologist who suddenly died. Shortly after death, he found himself in unfamiliar surroundings, and he was having trouble orienting himself.

While he was trying to establish his location, he saw an old, long-gone, respected colleague calmly floating by on a cloud. As the psychologist looked more closely, he observed that his old friend was seated next to a rather attractive, scantily dressed young woman. "I've got it," said the first psychologist. "I have died—and I'm now in heaven. That lovely girl there must be your reward!"

The second psychologist looked dowr from his cloud and sadly said, "No! You have it slightly confused. She's not my reward—I'm her punishment."

On their fifteenth wedding anniversary, Joe Brendon gave his wife Jan an expensive imported food blender. The machine was used twice, and now it stands neatly covered with plastic in the cupboard under the kitchen sink.

For his thirty-fifth birthday, Rod Silver received his own initialed bowling ball. To please Fran, Rod is using the ball each time he bowls—even though the weight is wrong.

When Mary Stevens was graduated from high school last June, her grandparents gave her a hair dryer to take to college. She had already received three others.

If you're like most people I know, you have also had the experience of being given the gift you didn't need or the gift you didn't want or the gift that someone else really couldn't afford. At other times, you must have fretted and worried about what you should buy for someone else.

As a psychologist, I have no objection to the giving of some well-chosen material gifts to those you love.

Indeed, toys can be terrific, and sweaters can be super. An

opal can continue to sparkle for many years, and the memories of a surprise winter vacation to a Caribbean island can warm one's thoughts during the rest of a bitter winter.

The delight that comes from a well-wrapped doodad is usually brief and shallow. The happiness and growth that can come from giving and getting a good *psychological* gift can be a source of continuous joy and increased emotional health. It's nice to give things that won't wear out or that won't further deplete our natural resources and that will continue to flourish and fortify.

Our actions count in our relationship with others. The lives of others are touched by what we do or don't do. An action of ours can be a seed that can grow into a rich source of emotional nourishment. Or, an unthinking action can become a weed that can crowd out another person's productive growth.

Like the ancient planter of carob seeds, try giving these very important emotional gifts to those you love. Your loved ones will be enriched—and so will you.

In our thing-oriented culture, we all too often equate giving with buying.

This faulty equation, at its best, adds up to temporary happiness. At its worst, it can multiply troubles and tensions and can instill false values in others.

Besides, the giving of bigger and better and more *material* gifts is a game that probably will not be able to be played by too many people in the foreseeable future. The end of that game would seem to be in sight.

❧

Don't tell the NN, but the world is beginning to run out of nonrenewable resources.

1. Every year there are millions of people born on this planet.
2. Every month we burn tons of coal.
3. Every day we use up millions of gallons of gasoline.
4. Every hour there are more and more people who want and need the same item. They need the same gallon of gasoline for the car, the same smidgen of gold for a telephone wire, the same piece of tungsten for a light bulb.

So the price of everything is going up all over the world. And there are fewer and fewer material things available for the more and more. The cherished American dream of children having more and bigger and better than their parents is about to turn into a nightmare. It's beginning to happen!

In 1950, *Fortune* magazine found that seven out of ten American families could afford to buy a new house. In 1975, only four out of ten families could manage to buy into the new housing market. Many Americans are living in homes they could no longer afford if they had to buy them today.

This all could make a confirmed NN so nervous that he might want to run out and buy a big, new car before they stop making them. After all, you have to take care of Number One, don't you?

❧

The fact that we are running out of lots of material things may not be all so bad. It can help people realize that some of the most important joys of all cost very little and are often renewable.

Laughter wastes little energy, and walks in the woods don't cost very much. The sight of a sunset doesn't cost a cent—and smiles don't wear out!

As a matter of fact, smiles are strange. The more you try to give one away, the more others send back to you.

An awareness of the shortage of material resources can lead us to understand that this is truly one world that we share. What one person does affects the lives of others. The fallout from a nuclear explosion in China soon produces increased radiation in the milk of cows in Pennsylvania.

The confirmed NN's may have to take a long, hard look at how selfishness can harm others and themselves as well. This world has become too small for everyone to "do his or her own thing."

It's a little like the fable of the group of people crossing a deep river in a ferryboat. Halfway across, one of the passengers decided he would drill a hole in the floor of the boat.

"What are you doing?" shouted the other passengers, who became alarmed. "What do you care?" the man replied. "I'm drilling the hole under *my* seat."

2. The Gift of Time

There's a time for some things, and a time for all things; a time for great things, and a time for small things.

—Miguel de Cervantes, *Don Quixote*

To GIVE SOME TIME to those you love can be a wonderful gift. Time is a very precious commodity. It is a nonrenewable resource; once a moment is spent it has gone to join all those other moments we call the past. The NN's have discovered the value of time, and most of them spend as much of it as possible—on themselves! Sometimes, there's nothing left over for other people.

A couple of years ago, I worked with a nine-year-old boy who was a severe behavior problem at school, in the neighborhood, and at home. In school, he was restless and fidgety and seemed not to be interested in learning. In the neighborhood, he was irritable and got into many fights with younger children. At home, he was negative and cranky and frequently complained about feeling sick.

His father was a successful lawyer who rarely was home. He didn't have time to spend with the boy. His mother was interested in "fulfilling" herself, and so she was a full-time student at college. The house was cared for by a series of housekeepers, who would stay in the home until they learned enough English to find a better job. After a few years of this routine, the boy learned how to make himself so unpleasant that each new housekeeper learned English faster than her predecessor!

Sometimes these parents, feeling a bit guilty about the lack of time spent with their son, would arrange a quick overnight trip to one of the many "plastic" amusement parks that have mushroomed during the past few years. During such a weekend, they would buy their son almost everything he wanted in a frantic attempt to atone for their lack of care during the rest of the year.

Weed ─────────→ He was given lots of toys, but he wasn't given time.

Happily, after many months of counseling, the parents came to understand how badly their son wanted some of their time. They came to understand that his frequent stomachaches were not stomachaches at all but were really attention aches. Unconsciously, this boy knew all along that if he were sick his parents would show care and give him time—and so he was on the road to becoming a chronic hypochondriac.

After a while, when both parents started to spend some more time with him, a marked change occurred. He complained less and became pleasanter to be with. As he became more agreeable, his parents began to enjoy him even more and desired to spend more time with him. His work in school improved, and he began to play well with friends.

Seed ─────────→ "Tincture of Time" can help!

❦

Psychologists who have studied the parent-child relationship know how vital it is to a child to have someone who gives time and care. When children receive a lot of time and care, they usually do well emotionally, socially, and intellectually.

It is perhaps for this reason that "only" children—in spite of the unfavorable stereotypes about them—tend to grow up to be strong, reliable, and healthy adults. In a recent study of only children, Dr. Toni Falbo, at Wake Forest University in North Carolina, studied a large number of only children. She compared the behavior of these children to firstborns, middle-borns, and last-borns.

The results of her study indicated that children are not necessarily "like peanuts"—and that sometimes "one can be enough." Most of the only children in her study seemed to be more independent and articulate and had a higher IQ than children who had brothers or sisters. Dr. Falbo speculated that only children might have done somewhat better because ". . . they spend more *time* with their parents during the formative years."

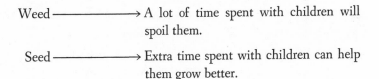

Weed ⟶ A lot of time spent with children will spoil them.

Seed ⟶ Extra time spent with children can help them grow better.

NN's are very busy with themselves—and taking care of children is seen as being square.

It's certainly important for parents to spend some time *away* from their children—but during such a period it's vital that a child is cared for by a responsible adult who truly cares.

Recently, the Cornell University child development expert, Dr. Urie Bronfenbrenner, commented, ". . . the question is, who *is* caring for America's children? The answer is disturbing. Fewer and fewer parents are doing their job of caring for children. Meanwhile, substitute-care facilities are in very low supply, at least in this country. They're expensive for those who can afford them and practically nonexistent for those who can't."

Weed ⎯⎯⎯⎯⎯⎯→ A parent must be with the children *all* the time.

Seed ⎯⎯⎯⎯⎯⎯→ A parent can spend *some* time away from a child so long as someone who *cares* is present.

❧

When you are dealing with children, it's also important to remember that although most of them walk to the tune of the same drummer, the beat of the music might be different.

Some children mature very early, and others take a little longer to travel the same road. One child may be ready to be toilet-trained at eighteen months. Another may not be ready until three years of age.

What a gift it can be if parents could hear the beat of their child's own rate of development and then try to adjust demands to meet emerging possibilities! It's all in the *timing!*

In my work as a practicing psychologist, I don't think I have ever seen a child with a reading problem who hadn't developed the problem because he or she was pushed to read before being ready. By being exposed to a difficult task before there is enough maturation, a child becomes doomed to failure! In most cases, if parents would just give the child a little more time, the child would be able to learn more easily.

Sometimes, when children are about two or three years old and beginning to speak, they may, in an effort to have the words come out just right, hesitate in their speech. An overanxious parent might say, "Now watch your words carefully. But don't hesitate so long."

Thus, a chronic speech problem can be created. Had the parent given the child enough time, a problem could be prevented.

Weed —————→ Children should be trained as soon as possible.

Seed —————→ Each child has his or her own time schedule that should be understood and used.

Relationships between adults can also be enriched if we respect the importance of giving time to the persons we love.

A few years ago, I began to work with a couple whose marriage was in serious trouble. He, the son of a poor country doctor, had grown up during the Depression. He devoted almost all his time to an everexpanding hardware store. She, the daughter of a professional Navy officer, did not expect very much time! She got even less! After several years of marriage, she came to resent his devotion to nuts and bolts and his lack of time at home. In twelve years of marriage, they had gone out together no more than a handful of times. Slowly, she came to resent her position on his list of priorities. At this point, she urged him to come for counseling.

After about five weeks in treatment, she had a routine appointment with her gynecologist, who made an alarming, unexpected discovery. He found a lump on her breast, and she had to have a biopsy. Analysis of the tissue revealed that she had a highly malignant cancer that had, in all probability, spread throughout her body. Her doctors held little hope for long-term recovery.

Almost immediately after the surgery, her husband became terrified about losing her—and he began to involve himself with her in every way possible. They went out to dinner; they attended the theater; they planted a row of hedges. Confronted with death, they began to live. He suddenly found enough *time* for her.

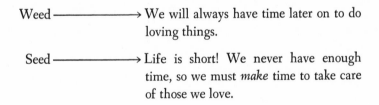

Weed ⟶ We will always have time later on to do loving things.

Seed ⟶ Life is short! We never have enough time, so we must *make* time to take care of those we love.

Often, even in the most intimate relationships, a lack of patience can create many problems. Careful and conscious giving of the gift of time can often work wonders.

Believe it or not, that's what a lot of the new sex therapy is all about. Yes, it's about time. Plain old time.

Drs. Masters and Johnson in St. Louis have found that many couples begin to have sexual difficulties when they become impatient with either themselves or with each other.

A typical case may go something like this:

Robert N., age fifty-two, has been impotent for the past two years. His problems began gradually after he noticed that it took him longer to get aroused. His wife, in a joking manner, said, "I guess you're getting old—or are you seeing someone else?"

Robert soon became increasingly upset and impatient with both himself and his wife. She, in turn, became increasingly upset and unsure about herself.

Had Robert and his wife been familiar with pioneering work in sexual functioning, they would have known that it's perfectly normal for male sexual arousal to slow up a little bit with increased age. With a little bit of loving *time,* however, gratifying sexual activity can continue into the eighth or ninth decades of life.

It took awhile for Robert and his wife to understand that they should take some *time.* When they did, sex again became gratifying. Yes, time can heal and help!

If too many major changes are made within a short period of time, psychologists have learned that we become more vulnerable to *dis-ease.* (Literally, we become uncomfortable.)

Research has shown that it's important to try and space major life changes over a period of time and to remember that we shouldn't try to do everything all at once. If, during the span of a year, we buy a new house, change jobs, have a baby, and take on a new, heavy financial burden, we are asking for trouble. Most people simply can't handle this much change in a short time span.

Weed ——————→If you *try* hard enough, you can *do* anything.

Seed ⟶ Given a little time, you can probably do much better.

Weed ⟶ It's good to get everything done at the same time.

Seed ⟶ It's best to give oneself some time to adjust to major changes.

❧

In a close relationship, caring people give the other persons time to be themselves and time to adjust to change. Each of us has a different breaking point, and each of us has to work through feelings and distress situations at our own rate and time.

One husband, for example, was initially very sympathetic with his wife when her mother died. Having always had an extremely close relationship with her mother, Helen, thirty-five, was shocked and almost numb after she learned that her mother had died suddenly.

During the funeral, and for a couple of weeks afterward, Helen's husband was concerned and understanding. After three weeks had passed, however, and Helen's grief did not seem to lift, he became gruff and harsh. "Why don't you snap out of it? It's gone on too long," he demanded. "If I could, I would!" she replied. "Let me alone. I just can't get over it just yet."

Frustrated and angered by his own inability to relieve Helen's grief, he became sullen and morose. He did not give her the time that she needed to mourn the death of her mother.

Other people simply do not react the way we expect them to. They react the way they *need* to react. That's important to remember. Very important, indeed!

Although everyone knows that people need to grieve after a catastrophe, it's important to know that they do so in their own good time. They don't necessarily follow the route we have outlined on our own road maps.

A few years ago, a terrible tornado caused considerable damage to Worcester, Massachusetts. Shortly after the disaster, a team of scientists, who were working on a project for the government that was designed to study the behavior of people following severe disasters, flew into Worcester.

In interviewing many survivors of the tornado, they arrived at some interesting conclusions. One of the findings was that many of the people who were exposed to the tornado functioned perfectly well during the disaster and its immediate aftermath. One to two days later, however, many of these people experienced emotional collapse and for a period of time couldn't function at all.

Weeds ⟶ Feelings follow a predictable timetable. If a certain feeling isn't resolved in a brief period of time, it means that there must be some severe problem.

Seeds ⟶ Feelings are not like scheduled airlines. They do not arrive and then depart on schedule. We should give those we love time for their feelings to arrive, time for them to stay as long as they need to, and finally time for them to depart.

Almost three-quarters of a million Americans die of heart disease every year. Can you imagine that? Three-quarters of a million people! Why, that's enough people to fill up a sizable city.

Cardiologists know that there are many reasons why some people develop and either survive or succumb to heart disease.

Cholesterol, diet, heredity, and cigarette smoking would all seem to play a role in this major health problem.

In recent years, however, many cardiologists have begun to focus their attention on another factor that seems to be involved in heart disease. That factor would seem to be personality!

Many cardiologists have come to believe that a person who is susceptible to coronary artery disease is likely to have a very special type of personality. They have even given that personality a name. It's called type A.

Psychologists have found that type A personalities, in addition to their obsession with success, are also constantly racing the clock. It's like everything they do—it should have been done yesterday. And everything that was done yesterday should have been completed six months ago.

It may be tough for *us* to race the clock, but it's even tougher for our arteries.

During peak levels of time-pressure, all sorts of physical changes that might precipitate coronary artery disease take place.

One study of accountants, for example, demonstrated that their cholesterol zoomed up from normal levels in early spring to dangerously high levels during the first weeks of April—in anticipation of the April 15 tax-filing deadline. As this target date for most Americans passed, the accountants' cholesterol level fell back to normal.

If you're involved with type A persons, try to give them the gift of time. Do whatever you can to

a. help them slow down.
b. help them relax.
c. involve them with something outside of work.
d. take some time for physical activity.

The planter of the carob seeds took *time* to plant. Yes! Time can be a very great gift.

Some Extra Seeds

1. Just "being" with someone can be a great comfort to them.
2. Learn to live in the present. If you spend too much time in the future or past, you'll become tense.
3. Each moment of time has its own value. You can use it to help someone.
4. It's important to acknowledge past unhappiness—but then you have to use it to enrich the present.
5. It's important to plan for the future—at the same time that you live for today.
6. No one is ever *too* busy to call loved ones to tell them they are loved.
7. Older people, particularly, appreciate the gift of a brief visit.
8. You can help someone you love take the time to relax.
9. Making people wait for you by being constantly late for appointments can be a sign of contempt. Can't you give them the gift of promptness?
10. Do you know that everyone has a biological time clock? Yes! You and the people you love are to some extent controlled by a biological rhythm that can govern moods and efficiency. So give others time to get over a sour mood or an inefficient period.
11. When someone you love makes you angry, can you take some time-out before you blow up?
12. Mostly, caring is best given to another person by using the currency of time.

3. The Gift of a Good Example

Do but set the example yourself, and I will follow you. Example is the best precept.

—Aesop, *The Two Crabs*

According to legend, a wise mother eagle had to fly across a very wide river. Unsure as to the strength and flying ability of her two young children, she decided it would be prudent to ferry them, one at a time, across the broad expanse of water.

As she carried her first youngster across, she asked, "When I get old and weak, will you carry me across the river, just the way I am carrying you?" The young eagle replied, "Why, of course, Mother!"

The mother was disturbed by the rapidity of the reply.

She then returned to the other side of the river and began to transport her second child. Once again she asked, "When I get old and weak, will you carry me across the river, just the way I am carrying you?" This second young eagle replied, "Mother, I don't really know what I'll do when you are old and weak. I do know though, that when *I* am a mother and my children are young, I will carry them across this river just the way *you* are carrying me now."

The wise mother eagle was content!

Several weeks ago, I began to work with a twenty-five-year-old schoolteacher who was anxious and afraid of almost everything. She worried about doing a good job in the classroom. She worried if people would like her. She worried about getting sick. She even worried a lot about being so worried all the time. During one session she remarked, "You know, I'm just like my mother. She worries just the way I do. Do you think I learned it from her?"

Yes! In recent years, psychologists have come to realize that many of our emotional attitudes are learned, not so much by what others tell us, but by a process of imitating someone we love.

This young woman had learned from her mother to see the scary possibilities in every new situation. When she was young and would go to a birthday party, she remembered her mother anxiously asking whether there were any children there who had colds. When she was a little older and took swimming lessons, she recalled that her mother would usually be more interested in whether the pool was properly supervised than in finding out how much the girl had learned. As a teenager, she was scared by her mother's stories of girls who were raped because they stayed out too late or went to parties when the parents weren't home.

Weed ⟶ Worries are contagious.

In my work as a psychologist, I have learned that when the chips are down, most people do not do what we tell them to do. Most of the time they do what they have seen us do. They imitate! They observe! They model themselves after us!

※

Being a model for other people's behavior is quite a heavy responsibility. But, like it or not, other people are influenced by our actions.

A few years ago, a noted psychologist conducted an experiment that has since become a classic in psychology.

Dr. Solomon Asch, at Princeton University, would ask a student to judge the length of a line. When the student was surrounded by others who expressed the judgment that the line was longer than it actually was, the student tended to see the line as being longer! When the student was exposed to opinions that the line was shorter, he or she tended to judge the line as being shorter. The students did not consciously realize that their own judgment of the line was being affected by the judgment of others. But it was!

Do you know you have the power to influence the actions and decisions of others? Yes, you do! *Whatever you* do sets some sort of an example for *others*. Even if they don't realize it, *you* are *affecting their* behavior.

Just the way that a stone thrown into a lake will produce a series of little waves that will spread over a large area of the lake, so too is an action of yours likely to produce some "ripples" that will affect others.

A tuning fork that is struck and begins to vibrate will cause another tuning fork to vibrate at the same frequency. Even if you tell it not to!

I once worked with a thirteen-year-old boy who was in trouble because of repeated incidents of shoplifting.

The first time that the boy stole a tape from the local record store, he was let go with a mild warning not to do it again. The second time he stole a tape, the owner of the store called the police, who strongly admonished him not to steal anymore. The third time the boy shoplifted, he was taken to court. The judge ruled he could be placed on probation if the family would get him some psychological help.

During several family sessions, the father kept trying to lecture the boy on the importance of honesty. Sometimes he spoke quietly. Sometimes he yelled. Sometimes he threatened. The boy listened a lot and said very little.

During one session, I began to try to find out about the boy's interest in tapes and stereos. When we hit on that topic, he became more animated and began to talk about himself and his interest in electronics. I learned that he played the piano. I learned that he had a collection of more than two hundred tapes. I also learned that his father had bought him his present tape deck. But, *now get this,* his father had bought the tape deck— not from a store—but from a truckdriver who worked for a large discount appliance outfit. The driver told the father he would make a special deal but he didn't want to be asked too many questions. The truckdriver sold the boy's father the tape deck at a very reasonable price! Very reasonable, indeed!

Weed ————————→ Children will not always do what we tell them to do.

Seed ──────────→ Children are more likely to follow our
example.

🌻

Many NN's don't like the fact that what they do affects the actions and feelings of others.

They would like to continue to do as they please, and yet have their children grow up to be the kind of people who would return glory to their parents. They would like their children to be superstars. It's a little like wanting a bank to give you a lot of interest on a very small investment.

Most of the time, it simply doesn't work out that way.

1. "My husband and I are very upset about our daughter. She shouldn't be sleeping around the way she is at fourteen. Just because *we* have an open marriage doesn't mean that *she*. . . ."
2. "I want him to stop smoking pot. I don't care if it is going to be legal soon. It can't be good for him. My wife says *I* should get some help with my drinking problem but. . . ."
3. "He should stay in school! What will he do if he leaves at sixteen? I know I left school when I was sixteen, but that was different."

Seed ──────────→ You can't condemn children for doing
what you have done or have been doing
all along!

🌻

Anger would seem to be a normal emotion that arises whenever some need of ours becomes thwarted or frustrated. Handled correctly, anger can be the fuel that can stoke the furnace of effective action. Handled poorly, anger can result in senseless destruction or impotent rage.

If children are exposed to models of excessive physical violence, they are likely to follow this poor example and are likely to hurt and harm others at the slightest provocation.

A few years ago, for example, the Surgeon General's Office in Washington conducted an extensive study into the effects on children of the extraordinary amount of violence to be seen every day on television. The principal investigator of this study was a very able psychologist, Dr. Robert Liebert.

Dr. Liebert carefully compiled the results of more than fifty studies that involved more than ten thousand American children. He concluded that "the more violence and aggression children see on television, regardless of age, sex, or social background, the more aggressive are they likely to be in their own attitudes and behaviors."

A friend of mine was playing golf with his ten-year-old son when a loud and pushy foursome began to crowd their game. My friend, politely but firmly, asked the group to give him and his son a bit more time. His calm assertiveness was rewarded. The rowdy group apologized for their behavior. They—and my friend's young son—had been given a good example to follow— a good lesson in the mature way to handle a situation.

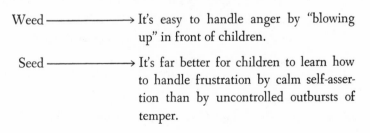

Weed ⟶ It's easy to handle anger by "blowing up" in front of children.

Seed ⟶ It's far better for children to learn how to handle frustration by calm self-assertion than by uncontrolled outbursts of temper.

❧

In this pleasure-oriented, do-it-for-me-because-I'm-the-only-one-that-counts period in our history, courage has become almost a dirty word!

Wrongly associated with skydiving or the single-handed capture of dangerous muggers, courage is too often relegated to heroes and heroines. Thus, we disown the potential for courage that exists within all of us.

Few of us today require the kind of courage that was once needed to guide a Conestoga wagon across a hostile prairie. All of us, however, could use the kind of courage that will guide us across a period of time in which the old historical road markers seem to have crumbled. Our tested values are being ridiculed and the NN's tell us that they are antiquated.

What has happened to us? What happened to the kind of moral fiber that Louis Adamic described as being "a certain blend of courage, integrity, character, and principle that has had no satisfactory dictionary name but has been called different things at different times in different countries?"

We no longer need the kind of courage that will disarm twelve attacking desperadoes. (We should call the police instead.)

We no longer need the kind of courage that we might have to use to perform emergency surgery in the middle of the night. (We should telephone for the first-aid squad to come with the rig and take the patient to the hospital.)

We no longer need the kind of courage that was required to have a tooth pulled. (We should tell our dentist we need another shot of Novocain.)

We all need, however, more of the courage that helps us understand that we almost always have some degree of *choice!*

Yes, we can always *choose*. We may not always choose a particular predicament that we find ourselves to be in, but we almost always have some degree of choice as to how we *handle* that predicament!

We can, for example, choose to be kind, or we can choose to be unconcerned with the feelings of others.

A few years ago, Dr. Stanley Milgram at Yale University conducted a series of experiments in which he asked some of the subjects in the experiment to be deliberately cruel to others. Many of the students, in an effort to please their professor, followed his instructions. Other subjects, however, chose not to hurt another human being.

When we begin to become aware of the enormous power of choice that we have, we can start becoming the person we chose to be.

When we have the courage to do that, even terrible situations can be turned into opportunities to help and care for others.

Weed ⟶ You have no choice in what happens to you. Everything is just a result of your luck.

Seed ⟶ Luck is important. But even if our luck is bad, we always have *some* degree of choice.

❧

Several years ago, I worked with a very nice woman who had lots of problems. After much time and much hard work, some of her problems began to resolve themselves. But she wasn't feeling better very long before a new and bad problem threatened to undo all the psychological progress she had made. She suddenly found herself becoming hoarse when she spoke a lot. Soon she found that she was hoarse all the time. She became frightened because she had been a very heavy smoker, so she went to her physician, who referred her to a surgeon, who operated. He had to remove her larynx! For a few days after surgery, she was plunged into deep despair and rage.

Her surgeon, sensing her depression, asked a former patient of his—who had also had to have her larynx removed—to visit my patient.

The visitor explained to my patient that she was a member of a club called the Lost Cords. Members of this group had had the experience of needing to learn to speak by expelling swallowed air.

For a day or so, my patient was reluctant to even consider relearning speech. She was in a sulk, and she was angry at the hand of cards that life had dealt to her.

When she became aware of the pain she was causing those she loved, she made some very important decisions.

1. She decided to stop wallowing in self-pity.
2. She decided to be grateful for the fact that her surgeon had probably saved her life.
3. She decided not to act like a spoiled child who didn't get her way. She realized that it didn't make any sense to take out her anger on those who were trying to help her.
4. She decided to focus on what she *could* do rather than on what she *couldn't* do.

As a result of her very conscious and wise choices, she

1. began to cooperate in her rehabilitation.
2. started to cheer up her worried friends and relatives.

36

3. learned how to talk again.
4. visits other patients who have just had similar surgery.

Most important of all, this lady became a model to many other people who needed to see how courage could overcome some bad luck.

Seed ⟶ Even bad situations can bring with them the opportunity to give others the gift of a good example.

❧

Shortly after I received my degree in psychology, I donated some time to a clinic that tried to help severely retarded children.

We had a good staff at this clinic, and they all did what they could to help children who were brought to us. The social workers would take useful family histories. The pediatricians would evaluate any current health problems. The psychologists would estimate the child's intellectual potential and emotional problems. The psychiatrists would try to help establish a diagnosis and give suggestions for treatment.

Social workers, psychologists, and psychiatrists came and left. For some, I guess, it wasn't very gratifying to work with some of these youngsters whose future seemed to be almost hopeless.

In the comings and goings of the staff, I remember one psychiatrist very well. No matter how severely impaired a child would be, this psychiatrist would always come up with *some* suggestion that would build on a child's strengths. He never focused on a child's "couldn'ts" but always spoke about a child's "coulds."

Once he helped the staff understand that a very severely retarded eight-year-old could probably be helped to learn to tie her own shoelaces if someone worked with her.

Another time, he helped the staff understand that if the parents of a twelve-year-old boy would handle him differently, the boy probably could be toilet-trained and then he could attend school.

Most of all—he became an *example* for me!

Because of this man's example, I almost always try to find a person's strengths, rather than the weaknesses. He helped me to become a better psychologist, and I don't think he ever knew that he did!

Weed ⟶ Doughnuts have big holes!

Seed ⟶ Did you ever see all that dough around the hole in a doughnut?

In 1964, a young woman by the name of Kitty Genovese was killed as she was returning home from work. Though many people witnessed her brutal death, few went to her assistance.

The NN's weren't too concerned—after all, her murder didn't concern them. They were still alive! Life is for the living. Right?

But her death was not completely in vain, because after she died many people started to become concerned about the how's and why's of bystander apathy.

—After Kitty Genovese died, many papers all over the country wrote editorials about her death.

—After Kitty Genovese died, many people started to wonder

38

what had happened to our ability to be concerned about others.

—After Kitty Genovese died, many psychologists began to study bystander apathy.

A great number of the studies done by psychologists were quite clever. Some had "stooges" who would pretend to faint on a crowded subway car for the purpose of finding out who would come to the aid of the make-believe victim.

Other psychologists' stooges would have a make-believe seizure in an office building to find out who—and under what conditions —people would come to the aid of the victim.

Many of these studies had different results. Most of them, however, agreed on one point. *If bystanders do not see other people coming to the aid of a victim, they are not likely to come to the aid of that person, either.*

Once again it's the example that *others* set for us that, to a large extent, determines *our* behavior.

Once again it's the example that *you* set that, to a large extent, determines the behavior of *others!*

❦

Preaching to others doesn't help much. A good example does! Many years ago, the wry Frenchman, La Rochefoucauld, observed that "old people like to give good advice, as solace for no longer being able to provide bad examples."

Seed ⎯⎯⎯⎯⎯⟶ Your actions are always more influential than your words.

The other day I saw a car that had a funny bumper sticker on it. The bumper sticker read, "Insanity is hereditary. Parents catch it from their children."

You know something—there's something to that.

A family is a *unit,* and everyone sets an *example* for everyone else. If children go through a period when they are wild, they can upset their parents. If parents go through a period when they are wild, they can upset their children.

Weed ⟶ *Your* example can help other people go crazy!

Seed ⟶ *Your* example can help other people go sane!

A few years ago, Dr. Stanley Coopersmith studied the question of self-esteem. He tried to find out why some children had a high sense of self-esteem while others had problems with their sense of self-esteem and did not think much of themselves. Dr. Coopersmith learned that children with a good sense of self-esteem came from homes in which the parents had set *examples* of clear and explicit standards. These children, growing up in no-nonsense homes, were able to obtain a sense of self-esteem by overcoming obstacles and by achievement.

There's a well-known hospital that has as its motto the words "Go thou and do likewise."

The planter of carob seeds gave us an example. The right examples can be a very great gift.

Some Extra Seeds

1. Your behavior can always be a source of inspiration—or embarrassment—for those who love you.
2. You can be very poor financially, but you can leave a rich legacy of example.
3. It's important to demonstrate to children how they can deal with anger.
4. It's important to demonstrate to children how they can deal with fear by moving through it.
5. Do you know that you almost always have *some* choice in a situation? Can you use that moment to set an example for someone you love?
6. Can you help other people by sharing with them some of the problems that you have overcome?
7. You can help those around you by being the first to pitch in.
8. Your children will remember more about the way you *did* things than what you *gave* them.
9. One good example is worth more than a thousand words.

4. The Gift of Acceptance

Things cannot always go your way. Learn to accept in silence the
minor aggravations . . . with an extra draught of hard work, so that
those about you may not be annoyed with the dust and soot of your
complaints.

—SIR WILLIAM OSLER, *Life of Sir William Osler*

ANCIENT GREEK LEGEND tells the story of Procrustes, a wicked
and demanding giant. Procrustes had a bed into which he tried
to fit everyone who came to visit. Individuals who were too tall
would have their feet cut off so that they would fit. Those who
were too short would have their limbs stretched.

Unfortunately, many people try to force those they love into
a preconceived mold that may not fit a loved one at all!

In our fast-moving, "fix-it-quick" or "make-it-better" society,
the NN's try to force everyone close to them into a Procrustean
existence. As a result of their concern with external appearances,
the NN's sometimes treat people around them as if they were
pieces of furniture that could be moved about and reupholstered,
restored, or remodeled whenever the need arises.

Several months ago, I worked with a couple in their mid-
thirties. He was a successful lawyer; she, the manager of an

exclusive boutique. They had three lovely children and a fashion-plate home. He was a confirmed NN and spent much time each weekend selecting the right pair of slacks to wear to the golf club.

Since their marriage, now ten years old, he had derived much pleasure from the compliments his attractive and vivacious wife received when they went out together or when they entertained some of the local NN's. How clever he was to have chosen such a pretty woman! How wise he was to have picked a woman whose physical appearance complimented his own!

One day, he noticed she had developed some crow's feet under her eyes! As the crow's feet deepened, his admiration began to shrink and, after a few months of unspoken concern, he decided to share his discontent with his beloved. She consulted a very fine plastic surgeon to find out what could be done. The surgeon suggested that there was no indication for surgery, and that the kind of complicated and painful surgery that would be required should be reserved only for people whose appearance was markedly impaired.

Not content with this opinion, the husband urged his wife to arrange for another consultation. However, instead of seeing another surgeon, his wife arranged a consultation with a psychologist. She wanted to know why she ever married someone like that!

Weed ⟶ We should try to change those we love to suit our image of what they should be.

Seed ⟶ Most of the time, people around us have their own notions of what *they* want to be.

43

❦

As a practicing clinical psychologist, I know from my work with people—as well as from research findings—that acceptance of others is often the best way to help open the door of change!

When we prod, insist, cajole, or try to force others into doing what *we* want them to do, they often become *more* resistant to change. What a gift it would be to those we love if we would only *accept* some unpleasant aspect of them long enough to let *them* decide that it's time to change!

Many problems between husband and wife or between friends begin when one person tries to change the other. But, did you know that people begin to shed bad habits once they are accepted the way they are? I know a man who had been over-weight since childhood. When he was young, his mother scolded him about his weight. When he married, his wife nagged him at mealtimes! Then, two years ago, his wife realized that she had to accept her husband the way he was; she never mentioned the subject of weight again. Within a few months, the man put himself on a rigid diet and has maintained a normal weight for more than a year.

Weed ——————→ "You really should lose a few pounds."

Seed ——————→ "I love you."

Weed ——————→ "You have been drinking much too much lately."

Seed ——————→ "I like you."

Weed ——————→ "You always embarrass me when you tell that stupid story in company."

Seed ——————→ "I respect you."

❦

In my work with parents and young children, I often find that a child's emotional development can be crippled when the child's parents try to force him into patterns of behavior that simply are wrong for that particular child.

All too many current articles in magazines, guides to child-rearing, and the treatment of children's problems in the movies and on television subtly suggest that *all* children are the same. They seem to say that if parents will only handle them properly and read enough child psychology books, each child can be molded by experienced parents and teachers into an individual who will always be happy, never experience anxiety, and will be able to glide through all of the vicissitudes of life like a hot knife cutting through butter.

Sometimes, I think that if all the articles and books that are intended to be *specific* guides to child-rearing were laid end to end—it would be a good thing.

I get upset when I see NN parents desperately trying to force their young children into some "norm" or "average" they read about in last week's Sunday supplement.

Norms and averages and statistics certainly have a place in psychology. The problem starts when we try to squeeze or stretch a child so he'll fit into the norm. Anyway, statistics describe a *group* not an *individual!*

During recent years, some solid, well-conducted research studies of children have concluded that many very basic personality traits are probably inherited. Some children, for example, seem to have a high need for activity. They like to move around a lot, and they need physical expression. Others seem to have less need for physical activity and appear to enjoy periods of quiet play.

45

Trouble can begin when we can't *accept* the very basic personality traits of our children.

I once worked with a young man who was having a very uncomfortable time accepting himself. He was a psychological mess!

He

1. was doing poorly in college.
2. had very low self-esteem.
3. was too shy to make friends.
4. couldn't accept himself!

When he was a child, his father, who had been a well-known football player when he was younger, tried to force the boy into athletics.

Now sports should be fun—not work! But because excellence in athletics was so important to this man, he started to teach his son much too soon!

—When the boy was three years old, he couldn't catch the football his father threw to him. It bounced off his arm and gave him a bloody nose!
—When he was six years old, he couldn't come down the steep ski slope. He sprained his ankle.
—When he was nine years old, he didn't want to join Little League baseball. His father made him. He struck out!

Weed ——————→ If we apply enough pressure, we can make our children into what we want them to be.

Seed ——————→ Each child has a unique personality. We can guide growth, but we can't force it.

Seed ⟶ If *we* accept children when they are young, they are likely to become *self*-accepting when they grow up.

Teenagers are tough to cope with. Most people can't stand them. NN's can't stand them even more than the rest of us.

Teenagers are usually hard to take because they are at a stage in their lives when they are sowing their oats and beginning to question authority.

NN's get insulted when their authority is questioned. How *dare* those kids question an NN?

So most NN's, in order to deal with the teenage plot to undermine authority, declare war on their teenagers and, when they do, they usually use one or two favorite weapons!

They either will *crack down,* or they will become overly *permissive.* And all too frequently the word *permissive* has become an euphemism for *neglect.*

I once worked with a teenage boy who was in bad trouble. He was failing in school; he had been in difficulty with the police; and he had stolen a car. When the parents came back from Europe, they found some time to come in to see me. When I asked them why they hadn't set some limits for the boy's behavior, the father replied, "Well, we are very permissive parents."

They weren't being genuinely permissive at all; they simply didn't care enough to get involved.

When parents do crack down on their children, they sometimes come down so hard that instead of eliciting cooperation they add fuel to the smoldering fires of rebellion.

For example, one girl had been "fresh" to her homeroom teacher, so the teacher wrote a note to her parents.

When the girl's father came home that night, he

1. took away her telephone privileges.
2. told her she wasn't allowed out of the house for a month.
3. removed the television set from her room.

She ran away with a boyfriend two days later!

When you are dealing with teenagers, an ounce of *acceptance* is often worth a pound of *punishment*.

In a recent study, for example, one psychologist found that when parents tried to break up a teenage romance, the romance was more likely to last than when the parents were more understanding.

Weed ⟶ Unless we crack down hard on teenagers, they will walk all over us.

Weed ⟶ We should always be permissive with teenagers.

Seed ⟶ If we can accept the fact that a teenager is in a tough stage, we might then find constructive ways to help.

❧

Last year, there were more than a million divorces in the United States. This year, there will be even more.

In my work with people who are having marital problems, I find that there's a rare (almost magical) ingredient that's often missing from a marital stew that's about to boil over. If this ingredient were to be added to the troubled cauldron, a boiling marriage need not spill into a fiery divorce.

This rare ingredient doesn't come from the Spice Islands. It doesn't come from Ceylon. It doesn't even come from a far-off land across the sea. It can be found right inside ourselves if we choose to look for it. It's called *acceptance!*

As a result of the ever-increasing collision between the promise and dream of marriage with its actual reality, many people slip into resentment or anger or fall into the trap of blaming one's mate.

Yet, acceptance of one's marital partner for better or for worse is the essence of the marriage contract.

I remember having had a consultation several years ago with a rather uneducated man who was in his late eighties. After having gone through a long siege with repeated surgery for a broken hip, he began to show some personality changes. His family physician referred him to me for psychological evaluation in the hope that I could shed some light on the reasons for these changes.

This man came to my office accompanied by his wife of sixty-seven years.

At one point during the interview, he became rather irritable with his wife and demanded, "What are you doing sitting there like a fool! Why don't you tell the doctor what he asked?" Embarrassed by his outburst, yet understanding what provoked it, his wife turned to me and said, "Pay him no heed, doctor. It's all the pain that he's been through the past six months that's talking now!"

Can you imagine what she would have been told if she had gone to a NN meeting?

"Get out! Don't let anyone *ever* talk to *you* that way."

"I would send him to a nursing home. Straight to a nursing

49

home. I wouldn't even wait to pass Go and collect the Medicaid payment."

"Get rid of him!"

❦

All too often, we try to "dump" blame for our actions on past events or on other people. Fifty years ago, psychologists placed great emphasis in the origin of people's problems. In the process, many people found it easy to cop out from personal responsibilities by wallowing in ancient history and past injustices.

Today, psychologists have become more interested in finding out where you can *go* rather than in learning where you have *been*.

We have learned that although we can't always be held responsible for what we feel, we must always *accept* responsibility for what we do.

When we own up to the fact that all of us have feelings and desires and ideas of which we are not particularly proud, we can then choose to accept them as parts of our personality that have either not grown up or have not been completely civilized as yet. We all have a dark side to our personality, and sometimes I have found that the "bigger" a person is, the "longer" is the shadow that is cast.

When we cannot accept our own dark sides, however, we are likely to disown these feelings and, when we do so, we are likely to attribute them to someone else.

I once knew a man who was very cheap. He was so cheap that old Abe Lincoln would practically yell with pain before this man would let a single penny squeeze through his fingers.

Unfortunately, he didn't accept the fact that he was cheap.

As a matter of fact, he thought he was quite generous. So he kept accusing other people of being stingy!

Seed —————————→ We can accept others better when we start to accept parts of ourselves that we don't like.

❦

All too many people in our times play the "Being the Best" game. Caught in a trap of perfectionism, they keep raising the standards for themselves in a cruel and unmerciful way. People who are depressed are often people who cannot accept their real accomplishments, and their depression represents a heavy wet blanket of self-loathing.

Often, a case of severe perfectionism is contagious. First you have it—then you want to give it to everyone else who is close to you.

What a rotten gift to give to someone you love! Better save such gift for an enemy! Yet time after time I have seen parents who try to force a child into perfectionism, or a husband who tries to make his wife into an idealized version of what he would like her to be.

Weed —————————→ People could be perfect if they only tried.

Seed —————————→ Perfectionism is the worst enemy to happiness that I know of.

❧

Can you accept the fact that any relationship that truly "meshes" is sooner or later bound to "grind"?

Yes, wherever there's true closeness, there's bound to be some friction. Where we can accept friction as the other side of the coin of closeness, we can begin to have better relationships with others.

Some people, however, have a great deal of difficulty in accepting the fact that other people are simply not on this earth to meet our needs. It would be nice if other people would always act in the way we would like them to act.

Unfortunately, however, other people have the nasty habit of acting in the way *they* want to act.

One of the loneliest people I ever knew was a rather attractive, unmarried woman. In spite of the fact that she met many people, her relationships almost always ended in dramatic psychological disasters.

She would meet a man and "fall in love" with him. For a short period of time, the new relationship would go well, but sooner or later the boyfriend would do something that *he* wanted to do that didn't conform to her expectations.

—Once a boyfriend told her he was tired and cancelled a date.
—Another boyfriend took her to a local diner for dinner instead of to a nice restaurant.
—Still another boyfriend told her he wasn't particularly interested in seeing all her slides of the Grand Canyon that she had just arranged in her new projector.

How dare *they* not act in the way *she* had expected?
This girl, unable to accept the fact that her friends were not

placed in the world to meet her needs, collected injustices in the same manner that other people collect trading stamps.

Instead of collecting "Green Stamps," however, this young woman collected "Brown Stamps." When she would have enough of them to fill a book, she would then convert all these little injustices into one giant, all-consuming *grudge!*

No wonder she was lonely!

Seed————————→ When we begin to accept people the way they are, we open the door to better relationships with others.

🌼

The planter of carob trees accepted the fact that it took seventy years for a tree to bear fruit. Can you?

Some Extra Seeds

1. If we accept the fact that the road isn't always smooth, we are well on our way to smoothing out the road.
2. You can help people change by accepting them just the way they are.
3. Can you accept the fact that there are times when you can't do anything except accept?
4. If we accept the fact that life is always changing, we can live with change more comfortably.
5. Do you know that if you accept someone else's expression of anger, the person usually begins to feel less angry?
6. Do you know that unless you can accept failure, you're unlikely ever to find success?
7. Acceptance of another can lead to his or her acceptance of you.

8. Can you accept the fact that regardless of what we do, we can't always feel happy?

Don't tell the NN's about this last seed; it might provoke a temper tantrum!

5. The Gift of Seeing the Best in People

One ought, every day at least, to hear a little song, read a good poem, see a fine picture, and, if it were possible, to speak a few reasonable words!

—GOETHE

Question: How can one see a "fine" picture of someone close to us—when that person doesn't always seem to be so "fine"?

Answer: Psychologists know that you will see what you *expect* to see.

Let's do a little experiment. I want you to look at this little illustration of a wine glass. See it? Good.

Now, turn the page!

Now, I want you to look at this illustration of the profiles of two girls whispering to each other. See it? Good.

Yes, it's the same picture. It all depends on what you expected to see!

In my work as a psychologist, I am impressed by the capacity of people to be shaped by the expectations of those who are close to them. If you truly want to give those you love a very precious gift, try giving them the gift of seeing the very best in them! More often than not their behavior will move closer to your expectation.

Most of the time, prophecies made about people tend to be self-fulfilling. Without realizing it, parents, in talking to children, prophesize future behavior.

"You didn't take out the garbage again? I think you'll be a *bum!*"

"You got an A in spelling. That's great. I think you're going to be quite a *student!*"

"Stop complaining about the umpire's call! You're the worst *sore loser* I ever saw!"

56

"Grandma told us that you did a super job of taking care of the dog and the fish while we were on vacation. You're going to be a good *mother* when you grow up!"

Just the way that a director of a play casts people into certain roles, so do parents, often without realizing it, write certain scripts for their children. Most of the time, the children act out the roles that are assigned to them. After all, acting jobs are hard to find, and everyone wants to be included in the drama. So, if you're not cast in the role of the "good guy or gal," you might have to play the part of the "bad guy or gal."

Here are a few of the parts that are still open in the play. There are many more!

1. Nice Guy
2. Liar
3. Quiet Man
4. Pretty Lady
5. Wild Indian
6. Winner
7. Loser
8. Honest Stranger
9. Flimflam Artist
10. Martyr

Which parts do you think *your* children will play? Which ones are you "prompting" them for with your comments and your prophecies?

Many months ago, Bob, a depressed thirty-five-year-old executive, came to see me. He wanted to leave a very fine job in a bank in order to take a new job as a part-time tennis instructor at a newly built indoor-tennis club.

"Each time he seems to be getting there," complained his

concerned wife, "he shifts gears and decides he wants to do something else."

After several sessions of talking about his erratic career, Bob blurted out, "I guess my wife is right. Each time I start becoming successful, I get depressed. It's like I'm more comfortable when things aren't going well. I've always thought of myself as a *failure*, and I guess I'm doing everything possible to make that nightmare come true."

"You're a *failure*," his father would shout, after a poor report card. "You're a *failure*," he would scream after Bob got fired from his job as a paper boy because he forgot to deliver papers one afternoon.

Bob soon accepted the failure name, and in doing so he began to play the failure game!

Weed ————————→ You can get children to shape up by calling them names.

Seed ————————→ Children tend to become what we tell them they are.

❦

The capacity of a prophecy to become self-fulfilling has been clearly demonstrated by Dr. Robert Rosenthal. In one experiment, Dr. Rosenthal spoke to teachers prior to the opening of school in the fall. He named some of the children as "academic sprinters" who were likely to achieve, but he made no comment about the other children. In reality, he had chosen the children at random—they had previously shown no greater intellectual promise than the rest of the group.

Amazingly, those children who were labeled as having good intellectual potential fulfilled the prophecy. At the end of the year, when *all* the children were tested, they showed more evidence of intellectual gain and achievement.

In another experiment, conducted with a group of children from Philadelphia, it was found that children were more likely to swim when their swimming instructors were told that the children were "ready" to learn. The instructor's expectations for these children were likely to be fulfilled.

The NN's get angry at their children when they do something that doesn't reflect glory on their parents. And when NN's don't get their daily dose of glory, they start to call their children nasty words!

"Amy, you're *lazy!*"

"Fred, you're *rotten!*"

"Phil, you're a real loser!"

Weed ⟶ Sticks and stones may break our bones, but names can never hurt us.

Seed ⟶ An *arm* broken by a stone will heal in time, but a *spirit* broken by a harsh word can cripple someone forever.

I have noticed that we communicate our expectations about children not only by the names we call them, but also by the names and nicknames we give them.

Do you want an unusual child? You can increase your chances of having one if you give that child a very unusual name.

In one study of Harvard students, for example, it was found that students who had unusual names were more likely to be unhappy and were more likely to need psychological counseling.

I was once consulted by parents who were concerned about their nine-year-old daughter's inability to play well with other kids. She didn't seem to know how to share, and she wanted everything her own way. The name of this young girl? Victoria! While she was still an infant, her parents had begun to call her "Princess."

You, also, better watch out for the nicknames that you use with your children. They also convey the expectations that you have for them.

A young NN and his wife became unhappy with their son. They were unhappy because the boy became so unhappy that he couldn't concentrate on his school work and began to fail. (NN's don't like to have children who have problems.)

It seems that this boy had done everything well. He did everything so well, as a matter of fact, that his father gave him the nickname of Superboy!

It seems that Superboy's problems began when he was cut from the high school's football team. That's enough to make any kid unhappy. For Superboy, however, it nearly turned into a tragedy!

It's not so good to be a Superboy. You're much better off being a plain, regular, human being who sometimes makes mistakes and who sometimes has to deal with disappointments.

Sam Goldwyn is reported to have once complained to an acquaintance about the name that he gave his son. "Why did you call him John?" said Sam, "Every Tom, Dick, and Harry is named John."

Weed ⟶ "Let's call the kid Percy. It's an old family name, and besides he'll develop lots of character when he has to defend himself."

Seed ⟶ It's good to see the best in children, but if our expectations are *too* high, they are likely to get mad at themselves too frequently for comfort.

Bad is a powerful word. It is often the most misused word in family situations.

If Lisa cheats on an exam, she did a *bad* thing. *She* is not bad. If her parents keep calling her bad, she's really likely to feel that she can never do anything that's good.

Weed ⟶ Some people are *completely* bad.

Seed ⟶ Most people can do some "bad" things, but they can change.

Sometimes adults get scared by seeing the *problems* rather than the *possibilities* that a new situation can bring. It's good when we can begin to help those we love see the *best* rather than the *worst* in a situation. We might help them become happier.

How someone *sees* a situation will often largely determine how he or she will *feel* about that situation. Let's take getting older, for example.

In our overpsychologized American culture, there are all kinds of psychological crises that we are warned to *expect!*

61

If one reads some of the rubbish that's around, it would seem as if each stage of life brings with it a new crisis. We no sooner finish our adolescent crisis than we have to start to go to work on our identity crisis! We just about get that one squared away when we have to begin to cope with the middle-age crisis!

If you listen to some people's ideas, the middle-age crisis can be a very scary one. Very scary, indeed! Why, you could get empty-nest syndrome. You could even get a crisis with menopause.

Want to know something interesting? If you *expect* a crisis, you're likely to get it. If you don't view an event as a crisis, the chances are that it won't be one.

There's some evidence around that would suggest that if a woman expects the menopause to be tough, it probably will be. If a woman does not *expect* menopause to be a crisis, the chances are pretty good that it won't be all that bad.

How you feel about the normal process of aging depends on where you happen to grow up. Studies that have been done show that in Belgium and Italy sixty percent of a group of women who were polled agreed that the menopause meant the end of their attractiveness to men. In England, however, only nine percent of the women polled predicted such a dire outcome from menopause.

Do you know that in Germany the word for middle-age is hardly used? If the Germans do call people in that age bracket something, they are likely to use the word *Erwachsenealter.* Meaning? Mature adult!

If you're a Navajo, you just can't wait until you get to be old. Navajos see old age as a time when one can really enjoy the fruits of one's labor. No midlife depression here!

Don't tell the NN's (you'll scare them half to death), but a few wrinkles and crow's feet don't mean that there's no future happiness!

Seed ——————→ When you expect the worst, you're likely to get it.

Seed ——————→ When you can help others see the *best* in a situation, you have given a good gift.

According to early Greek mythology, Pandora, the first mortal woman sent to earth, brought with her a box. When she opened the lid out of curiosity, all human ills escaped into the world, leaving only Hope at the bottom of the box.

In later times, the story was told differently. The box was then said to contain blessings, which were thus secure for humans. By opening the box, Pandora lost them all except Hope.

I know that hope helps! *You* know that hope helps! Now even *scientists* are finding out that hope helps!

1. In a recent study at the University of Rochester, New York, Dr. George Engle investigated the relationship between feelings of hopelessness and illness. He and his associates concluded that helplessness and hopelessness can weaken an individual's resistance to physical disease.

2. In England, a group of researchers studied the effects of hopelessness and despair on one's state of health. They studied a group of 4,500 men whose wives had recently died. During the first six months of hopelessness and despair, the death rate of this group was sixty percent higher than that for a group of comparable men who had not experienced such severe loss. After six months, most of

63

these men were able to adjust to the difficulties of their new lifestyle, and their death rate returned to normal.

3. In South Africa, Dr. R. J. Burrell, a qualified physician, watched six middle-aged Bantu tribesmen as they were "cursed" by the tribal witch doctor. They were told, "You will die at sunset." Each did! An autopsy failed to reveal the cause of death. You can die from *hopelessness!* Yes, you can.

Once upon a time, there were two frogs who fell into a bucket of cream. It was a deep bucket, and as much as the frogs tried jumping they simply could not seem to escape. The one frog finally gave up, and drowned. The other, though terribly fatigued, said to himself, "Even though it seems hopeless, I have no choice but to keep jumping!" So he continued to jump and jump. When he was almost totally exhausted, and about to sink to the bottom, he found he was able to stand on a chunk of butter.

Some frogs know better than some doctors.

A woman I know was told that her teenage son had a severe emotional problem and would never be normal. That gloomy prognosis didn't fit in with the woman's positive belief in her son. She took him to several other doctors before she found one who agreed to help. Her son recovered and will be graduated from law school next June.

In life-and-death situations, false hope may be stupid, but no hope at all is absurd. Yes, where there is still life, there is *always* some ray of hope.

In recent years, there has been a spate of books and articles on psychology and medicine about how to deal with the dying. All these books and articles agree that it's important to tell the dying patient the truth. I agree! All these books and articles stress the importance of letting the patient know what to expect. I agree! Very few of these articles and books, however, mention that it might be helpful to let a very sick patient know that *sometimes*, not very often, but *sometimes*, a very sick patient will suddenly —and for no apparent reason—begin to recover. Yes—Recover!

Everyone knows cases like that, but hardly anyone likes to talk about them. It's a little bit like believing in miracles. (NN's don't believe in miracles—they believe in themselves!)

Several years ago, I worked with a woman whose mother got very sick. She got sicker and sicker, and her symptoms baffled her doctors. She was brought to a large teaching hospital and exploratory surgery was performed.

When they looked inside the body, they found she had a very advanced case of a highly malignant cancer. They took some tissue for a biopsy, and then they stitched her up and waited for her to die. They gave her some medication to keep her comfortable and started her on some chemotherapy (which they really didn't believe was going to work). She got weaker and weaker, and it looked as if the end were near. Toward the very end, a daughter who lived many miles away called her mother. She had good news for her. It seems that her husband had received a promotion and a transfer at work, and they would soon be moving back to their home town.

On the phone, the daughter asked her mother to help sew the drapes for the new house they would be buying. The mother was delighted with such good news. She told her doctor that she had to *live*—because she had to sew for her daughter. She began to eat; she began to gain weight. Three weeks later, she was discharged from the hospital. Six months later (and one pair of living-room drapes later) the doctors x-rayed her and found no evidence of her cancer. It went away!

The doctors wrote about her case in the journals. Nine years later, she is still well, and the last I heard she was busily sewing for her granddaughter.

It doesn't always end that way. Some day I bet it will! Each year, it's ending this way for more and more patients. As scientific research pushes back the barriers of the shadows of ignorance, more and more people will get well! (Don't talk about scientific research to most NN's. They find that much of it is so boring—all that counting and stuff!)

Meanwhile, the most important thing to know is that it CAN happen! If it happened to this woman, it CAN happen to someone else! So there's always hope! Yes! Always some faint, dim glimmer of hope. What a loving and health-producing gift it is to kindle and brighten the spark of hope in those you love!

Weed ⟶ "I'm a hard-nosed scientist. The prognosis looks very dim. There's nothing we can do!"

Seed ⟶ "I'm a hard-nosed scientist. The prognosis looks grim—but let's try."

If we give the gift of seeing the best in people, we don't give those we love "no-win" labels.

I once worked with a rather unhappy young woman who broke into sobs as she confessed that she was frigid. And, indeed, since her honeymoon—five years ago!—she had experienced very little sexual gratification.

When she told her story, I began to understand what had happened.

This woman, from a rather traditional middle-class home, had very little sexual experience before her engagement. She married a man who was sexually sophisticated, but emotionally naive. On the first night of their honeymoon, she found that, although she enjoyed sexual contact with her new husband, she was unable to have an orgasm. The tension of the wedding, the exhaustion of the plane trip, and the general excitement of the past few weeks simply did not permit total relaxation. After trying a bit, her fatigued new husband kissed her and said jokingly, "I love you a lot, even though you are frigid."

The next day, she tried not to be frigid. She got even cooler. The following day she tried twice as hard not to be frigid—and she became twice as unresponsive. The more she tried to overcome her husband's expectations of frigidity, the worse things became.

I wonder how things might have been for her if he had never opened his big mouth!

I didn't help this lady very much. I think it's because her husband didn't want to come in with her. He told her, "It's your problem—not mine. Anyway, zebras can't change their stripes. People can't change either."

Weed ⎯⎯⎯⎯⎯→ Nothing ever changes!

Seed ⎯⎯⎯⎯⎯→ When we love someone, we try to encourage their attempt to grow. We don't put them down!

❧

When we give the gift of seeing the best in people, we resist the urge to put people we love into little pigeonholes of classification. In my work with families, I find that many parents are overly eager to classify behavior. By doing so, they often feel they are praising a child. Sometimes, however, too many evaluative comments about a child's performance may cause that child to stake out a premature claim to a certain area of competency. Allowed to wait longer, the boundaries might become larger.

Recently, I worked with a troubled family. Mrs. Redmond, an anxious, tense lady, received little in the way of praise when she was a child.

Having suffered the sting of rejection, she was most eager to compliment each of her three boys. "Jim is our *athlete*," she said. "Mitchell is the *student*, and Alan is a fine *mechanic!*"

As I learned more about this family, I learned why many of the problems arose.

1. Jim spent endless hours playing ball when he should have been "batting" his books around.
2. Mitchell's overconcern with marks made him the class brain and didn't allow him the freedom to develop some social skills.
3. Alan's narrow interest in fixing things was a way of copping out of any academic, athletic, or social achievement.

Each of these children had become overly specialized before they had even tried their hand in general practice.

Awareness of the fact that much in life is uncertain can help a person resist the illusion of certainty that "pigeonholing" brings.

Overreliance on "expert" opinion or upon an expectation

bestowed by a psychological authority can sometimes add more troubles to an already troubled child. I'm always astounded when an anxious parent of an eight- or nine-year-old eagerly asks, "Is he college material?"

When I get asked this question, I usually confess that my crystal ball is out for repairs—and that our very young science of psychology simply has not progressed to the point that a prediction about an event ten years in the future will be accurate.

Sometimes, parents will understand what I'm trying to tell them. Sometimes, they leave in a huff and go to a fortuneteller!

❧

"*You're* just like Aunt Sara!"

"Well, *you're* just like Uncle Mike!"

"*You* got the bad genes—like your father."

"*You* have a big mouth—just like your mother."

Without realizing the full impact of our actions, most of us tend to identify people close to us with people who were significant in our past. Family resemblances may sometimes foster such hasty identifications. The same color eyes or a similar tilt of the bridge of the nose may lead to the erroneous conclusion that Margaret may wind up like Aunt Sara—or that she may wind down like Uncle Charlie.

Each person is *unique,* and with the exception of identical twins, no two peas ever came out of a genetic pod exactly the same.

As a therapist, I often have had to spend a considerable amount of time trying to convince a patient who is having a simple bout with anxiety that she is not having a breakdown as Aunt Sara did. . . .

Everyone—well almost everyone—has an Aunt Sara or an Uncle Charlie.

Sometimes an Aunt Sara or an Uncle Charlie may have not been negative figures but revered figures with whom one must identify. What a burden!

Most healthy people rebel against the prospect of competing with a peeling portrait. One articulate man proclaimed, "I'm me! That's who I am!"

Weed ⟶ Everyone is *just like* someone in the past.

Seed ⟶ Everyone is different, and it doesn't make much sense to make grandparents responsible for what's happening *now*.

Seed ⟶ Stop putting people into psychological pigeonholes!

Some Extra Seeds

1. You can choose to see the best or the worst in people.
2. When you see the best in people, they are likely to live up to your view of them.
3. Names can hurt a lot. If you can't resist using them, at least try good ones.
4. If you know we *all* have a tendency to make the cowboys the *good* guys and the Indians, the *bad* guys, we can deal with things in a more evenhanded way.
5. When in doubt, help people keep their hopes.
6. You'll be able to change things faster if you criticize deeds and not people.

7. If you want to help someone who's in trouble, think of the *possibility* and not always the *probability*.

8. IQ tests are fine, but they can't predict someone's future. Motivation is sometimes even more important than ability.

9. If you're going to have a baby, don't give it a freaky name (unless you want a freak).

10. In life, people either "grow" or they "constrict." In which direction do you want to help? Then go.

6. The Gift of Privacy

A man must not try to force his way into the personality of another
... the soul, too, has its clothing of which we must not deprive it....

—ALBERT SCHWEITZER, *The Light Within Us*

"Leave me alone!"
"Get off my back!"
"Mind your own business!"

All the above pleas for *privacy* are being heard in more and more American households as our respect for the rights of an individual to privacy has declined.

Too frequently, we tend to smother those we love with questions or with demands on their time. What a good gift we give when we allow those we love the right to their own private thoughts and the privilege of having their own unshared feelings.

In recent years, there has been tremendous emphasis placed on the ideal of togetherness, and many families measure the success of their family life by the amount of time they spend together. Some time shared together can be wonderful, but too much time spent together can destroy warmth and closeness.

An older couple I knew, for example, had a fine relationship for forty years of marriage. During all that time, their relationship continued to expand and grow. They had experienced some tough moments, but these rough times had actually helped bind their relationship together. Now they were caught in a crisis that threatened to shipwreck their marriage. Joe had retired!

For many years, Joe had looked forward to his retirement. He hadn't been particularly happy with his job at the insurance company, and he found that fighting the rush-hour traffic had become increasingly harder to bear.

For the first few weeks of retirement, Joe reveled in his new-found freedom. He slept late, he visited friends, and he started to help his wife with many of her domestic chores. After a period of time with this routine, his wife found the situation intolerable. She found it so intolerable, as a matter of fact, that she decided to get a divorce.

"I can't stand him in the kitchen," she complained. "Every time I turn around, he's under my feet. I don't have a moment of *privacy*."

Fortunately, Joe got the message, and he joined a health spa, where he spends a few hours each day swimming and talking with the other men. His wife now has her kitchen back to herself, and her loving feelings toward her husband are beginning to return.

In my work with other couples, I find that each couple has a unique relationship in which there's a delicate balance between togetherness and privacy. Too much of either good thing can destroy this balance and cause unhappiness.

Many of the husbands I work with are employed by companies that require them to travel. Sometimes, in helping these couples repair a tottering marriage, I will see them together. Sometimes, I see them separately. During the past few years, I have been impressed with the fact that a *little* travel can be helpful to a marriage, while a *great* deal of travel can often have a harmful effect.

One woman explained, "When Pete is away for a day or two, it gives me a chance to do some of the things I can't easily do when he's here. I write some letters and take care of the checkbook. I can also take as much time as I like in the shower. After a short trip, I usually can't wait to see him. If he's away for more than a couple of weeks, though, I feel differently when he returns. It's almost as if we have to get to know each other all over again."

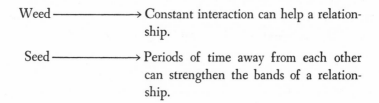

Weed ⟶ Constant interaction can help a relationship.

Seed ⟶ Periods of time away from each other can strengthen the bands of a relationship.

Many years ago, Thoreau wrote, "I never found the companion that was so companionable as solitude. We are for the most part more lonely when we go abroad among men than when we stay in our chambers. A man thinking or working is always alone, let him be where he will."

In my work with people, I've learned that periods of privacy are absolutely essential for problem-solving, for thinking, and for growing. It's during a period of privacy that people can come to terms with themselves! It's during periods of privacy that people can create!

We must have some private times if we are to expand our horizons or become aware of our deepest feelings.

NN's don't like to give the gift of privacy to others! No, NN's want someone else's attention *all* the time!

One NN husband, for example, made lots of happy noises in front of his friends when his wife went back to school to get her degree in social work. Why, it certainly was a feather in *his* cap to have a wife who was a professional.

Each time, however, that she would sit in the den and try to complete an assignment, he would go into a sulk. *He* wanted her to be around, when *he* wanted her to be around! *Her* needs for privacy were unimportant.

Your own need for privacy—and your need for contact with people—are highly personal matters. Some of you are able to enjoy the privacy of solitude. Others seem to need a lot of interaction with other people.

In recent years, psychologists who have studied the problems of privacy have learned that your own particular need for others is the result of many factors. In one study, for example, Dr. W. Denber found that firstborn children were more likely to seek out the company of others, whereas younger children tended to prefer going it alone.

Your sense of self-worth and security also plays a part in how much privacy you need. When you feel frightened and unsure of yourself, you are more likely to turn toward others in search of comfort.

Indeed, the very word *gregarious* comes from the ancient Greek word meaning *herd* or *flock*. In my work with people who are overgregarious and who cannot tolerate privacy, I often find a lot of unrealistic fear.

One middle-aged woman slowly began to need increasing amounts of social contact with others. Soon she could not even remain at home without her husband or a friend. Periods of privacy were avoided at all cost.

Afraid of getting old, this woman could distract herself only by the reassuring presence of others. When she began to resolve these unrealistic fears, she no longer needed people all of the time, and she began to relish periods of privacy.

> Seed ———————→ It's a great gift to be able to decide when those you love need companionship and when they want privacy.

❧

Psychologists know that we all live as if we are enclosed (and protected) by an invisible bubble of space. This bubble of space protects our privacy. Some people have rather large bubbles surrounding them, and people have to stay far away in order for them to be comfortable. Other people have smaller bubbles around them, and it's easier to get close to them. However, when our own personal *space* is invaded, we are likely to react with annoyance and discomfort.

Dr. Edward Hall found that the size of the bubble of space you need to be comfortable is mostly determined by your culture and background.

Americans, for example, seem to need a lot of space. When

Americans talk to each other, they seem to become uncomfortable if someone else comes within eight inches.

Europeans or Arabs, however, seem to have smaller bubbles, and people can come much closer to them before they start to give off signals that indicate their privacy is being invaded and that they are becoming uncomfortable.

Around any home, people also have areas of personal space. If you love someone, you respect these private areas of space and so you don't

1. put your sewing box on your husband's work bench.
2. open the Christmas card addressed to your wife.
3. borrow a dollar from your husband's wallet while he's taking a nap.
4. lend a book that you borrowed from a friend to another friend.

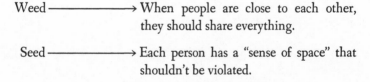

Weed ⟶ When people are close to each other, they should share everything.

Seed ⟶ Each person has a "sense of space" that shouldn't be violated.

Deed ⟶ Stay away from other people's space unless you're given an invitation to come in.

In his 1926 play, *The Great God Brown,* Eugene O'Neill did an interesting thing with masks. Each character in the play carries a mask in the style of the early Greek and Roman dramas.

When the characters in the play are unsure of themselves— because they are with a stranger or because they are anxious— they protect their privacy by using masks. When they become more comfortable with someone, they begin to lower the masks so that their real faces can be seen. Only with very few persons are the masks put down completely.

In real life, people also carry social masks. We all wear them and we all need them. There's no need for a casual acquaintance to know all about us. We should be the ones who choose the people with whom we wish to share a personal secret.

During the past few years, the encounter-group movement reached a peak, and now (fortunately) has begun to decline.

In an encounter group, a person was encouraged to talk about all feelings, hopes, aspirations, and fears to a group of strangers. It was thought that doing so would help individuals realize that their feelings and ideas were not terribly different from the feelings and ideas of others.

Encounter groups encouraged people to

1. let it all hang out.
2. tell it all.
3. not hold anything back.

Sometimes encounter groups worked, and a person felt a sense of relief at having made a public confession. A lot of the time, however, encounter groups boomeranged, and a group would cruelly attack a member for feelings that had been expressed. Sometimes, too, a kind of emotional "fascism" developed in which the group told a person what he or she *was* feeling.

Studies done of encounter-group "casualties" revealed that there was a surprising number of people who fell apart after having had an encounter-group experience.

It's not a pleasant experience to reveal your most private thoughts and experiences and then have others handle this information in a sarcastic or unfeeling way!

Weed ⟶ By helping people to get "everything out," they feel better.

Seed ⟶ It's important not to encourage people to tell more about themselves than they are ready to disclose. Everyone needs some privacy!

Suppose someone does tell you a secret. Do you know how to guard your friend's *privacy*? Can you resist the temptation to gossip?

I have found in my work with people that, for some individuals, gossip offers a tempting opportunity to feel superior. An unhappy person who feels small can soon feel "big" as he or she climbs the shaky staircase of rumor and broken confidence.

When someone gives you a special gift or a secret, it's only polite to repay it with the matching and equivalent gift of confidentiality.

When you are told a secret, you have been given a piece of private psychological property and you have no right to pass it on to anyone else. If you do, the results can be disastrous, not only for you, but for your friend as well!

The problems with gossip are that it is

1. not always accurate.
2. likely to get distorted as it gets passed from one person to another.
3. usually destructive.

A Case

Bill F., age thirty-seven, went on a business trip to New Orleans. While there, he was approached by a prostitute at the bar in his motel. Bill declined her invitation; but when he returned home the following week, he commented to his friend, Jim, "Wow, New Orleans is quite a town. I'm going to have to tell you about this girl I met."

Jim told his wife, "You know I spoke with Bill today. I never realized what a swinger he was. He apparently had quite a time in New Orleans last week."

Jim's wife was a close friend of Bill's wife, and so the next time they met, she said to her, "I really feel close to you, so I think there's something you should know. I found out from Jim that when Bill was in New Orleans, he was carrying on."

Needless to say, there was quite a hassle before things got straightened out.

Weed ——————→ You can help someone by passing on a piece of news.

Seed ——————→ A secret given to you is very precious. Put it in the safe-deposit box of your memory.

Deed ——————→ When in doubt, *shut up!*

❦

It's important to allow even a young child to have some privacy and space. When you do, the child can develop imagination and can muster resources so that he or she can deal with periods of solitude in a constructive and creative way.

Raymond V. was eight years old when he was brought to me by his anxious parents. Raymond was demanding at school and in the neighborhood. He constantly attempted to manipulate others into playing with him. By doing so, he became a first-rate pest.

When I saw him in my playroom, I was astounded to see the amount of attention he required. I couldn't take my eyes off him for a moment before he would demand my attention. When I gave him a piece of paper and crayons and asked him to draw a picture of a person, he couldn't do so without a barrage of questions.

"What kind of person should I draw?"

"If I draw stick figures, is it O.K.?"

"Should I use all the colors?"

When I interviewed Raymond's parents a while later, I understood what had happened.

Raymond's mother and father weren't sure they had wanted to have Raymond when he was conceived. They wondered whether or not there should be an abortion.

Finally, after a lot of thinking and some soul-searching they decided they wanted to proceed with the pregnancy. But even after Raymond was born, they weren't sure they should have had him.

Caught up in these conflicting feelings, they began to *overprotect* Raymond. They hovered over him and didn't give him a moment of *privacy*. Gradually, Raymond began to view all adults as if they were the social directors of his life. He looked to them for guidance in having fun.

Without adults, Raymond simply did not know how to entertain himself. He didn't know how to handle periods of privacy in a constructive way.

Weed ⟶ It's important to be with young children almost every minute.

Seed ⟶ Even young children can be helped by having some periods of privacy.

❧

Teenagers need a lot of privacy! It's a gift to let them have the privacy they need. Have you ever noticed how many teenage girls keep a diary? It's almost as if they need to write down some secrets so they can convince themselves they truly are individuals.

There's a bad myth around that tells us that teenagers *always* keep diaries because they want their parents to know what they are doing.

I don't believe that. I think that teenagers keep diaries because they want to have a sense of being grown-up and that they want to have their own secrets. And even if the diary is on a desk, I don't think anyone else should read it!

(Don't give me that stuff about her really wanting you to see it! Even if she does, you're just falling into a trap of indirect communication if you read a diary that doesn't belong to you.)

Letters written to teenagers should also be respected, even though the letters are left about in a rather casual manner.

Several months ago, I worked with a teenage girl and her family. She had lots of problems growing up. Her family had lots of problems in letting her grow up.

In order to demonstrate how her parents wouldn't let her be an individual, she would often leave opened letters from her friends around the house. Invariably, her parents would take the bait and read her letters. Then, they were caught in her trap of being parents who "won't let me grow up." And they were!

Weed ⟶ You have to check on the private areas of your teenager's life so you can be sure things are going all right.

Seed ──────────→ Teenagers, like everyone else, need some privacy so they *can* grow up to be all right.

NN's don't believe that teenagers or kids have the right to privacy! They believe that if a teenager *tries* to have some privacy, it's because he or she is doing something wrong.

❧

Some families become "ingrown." Like groups of cave people, terrified of dinosaurs, these families turn into themselves for protection, care, and assistance. Everyone *outside* the family is regarded as a potential, hostile stranger. Without any new friends, these families often become closed, seething crucibles of boredom.

Privacy, in this kind of family, is seen as an act of treachery, and every member of the family becomes dedicated to the proposition that everyone should "know everything about everyone else." If Cousin Lisa gets a boil, Amy calls Rhona. Rhona calls Aunt Anne, who calls Cousin Darra. Darra tells Lori, Lori tells Ira, Ira tells Jeremy. And so it goes until everyone in the family knows about the event.

Like primitive jungle drummers, who do not stop pounding their drums until the last distant outpost has heard the news, these families do not stop relaying a message until *everyone* in the family knows what has happened.

Often such a lack of privacy drives a member of the family to do something *very* private.

Recently, I worked with a man who did an interesting thing.

Twice a week—rain or shine—he went horseback riding. No one in the family knew where he was going or what he was doing. The more they became curious, the more guarded he became.

—His wife was sure he was having an affair.
—His mother and father-in-law (who lived upstairs) were sure he was having an affair.
—His brother and sister-in-law (who lived across the street) were sure he was having an affair.
—His mother and father (who lived two blocks away and were close friends with his in-laws who lived upstairs) were sure he was having an affair.

And he was!

He was having an affair with privacy!

🌿

Want to learn something odd?

Severely psychotic patients who are admitted to American mental hospitals seem to require much heavier doses of tranquilizers than do equally disturbed patients who are admitted to mental hospitals in Europe.

Recently, an expert in the use of tranquilizers, Dr. Heinz Lehmann, began to ponder about this situation.

Dr. Lehmann noted that, in Europe, a patient admitted to a hospital is likely to be placed in a quiet, secluded room in order to give the patient time to relax and to work out some problems.

In America, however, a newly admitted patient is encouraged to socialize with everyone. He's invited to go to group therapy and meet everyone on the ward. Dr. Lehmann comments, "I feel that if I had an acute psychotic episode, I would much rather be left alone and get the rest they get in Europe."

Yes, *we all* need some privacy now and then.

Some Additional Seeds

1. Do you know that everyone lives in a *private* world of experience!

2. If you want to understand someone, you can begin by respecting the person's individuality.

3. Do you know that only those who respect the *privacy* of others can begin to help them?

4. Consider: Twenty years ago, most students worked at individual desks in the public schools. Now many more public schools want their children to work at group tables.

5. Perpetual *openness* can be as dull as perpetual concealment.

6. Do you realize that boredom is really a state of misused privacy?

7. It's a good thing to let those close to you have a secret now and then.

8. Curiosity may have killed the cat, but I'll give you odds that for every cat it killed, it *maimed* a million relationships.

(Don't tell the NN's about all this. After all they have to find out about *everything* or they feel cheated!)

Yes, privacy is a very precious commodity in these times. Do you think that the carob tree was bugged?

7. The Gift of Self-Esteem

Oft times nothing profits more than self-esteem, grounded on just and right.

> —JOHN MILTON, *Paradise Lost*

I love you
Not only for what you are,
But for what I am
When I am with you.

> —RAY CROFT, in
> *The Family Book of Best-Loved Poems*

WHY, YOU KNEW that all along, didn't you? Some people make you feel good—and other people make you feel terrible.

The very presence of some people makes you feel high, as if you're on Mount Everest and headed for the peak! Other people make you feel low, as if you're on the bottom of the Atlantic Ocean and have to look up to see a whale's belly!

What strange creatures we are. We can make each other feel bad, or we can make each other feel good. We can boost or we can tear down another person's most precious possession. We can affect someone's sense of self-esteem.

As a psychologist, I know that perhaps the most fundamental need is for people to be able to feel good about themselves. Without a healthy feeling that "I count," nothing else can count for very much.

So much—oh, so very much—of people's behavior is designed to help them recover a lost sense of self-esteem, and much behavior is directed toward restoring a badly damaged sense of self-esteem. Sometimes a person's *whole* life is spent in the compulsive, relentless attempt to repair damaged self-esteem.

I have a patient, for example, whose mother was widowed when she was very young. In order to support her growing family, the mother had to take a job sewing coats in a factory. She was paid for each coat she sewed, so in order to make enough money to pay the rent, she worked twelve to fifteen hours a day. As a result, she had little time to clean the house, and their small home soon fell into disrepair.

One day, when my patient was seven years old, she had some friends over to her house for a birthday party. She heard one of her friends comment to another, "What a dirty house! Let's not come here anymore!"

The sense of shame that she felt—and the blow to her sense of self-esteem—were indelibly impressed upon her young mind.

My patient was like a young calf, whose hide is branded. Her sense of self-worth was severely and permanently scorched.

Now, when she is thirty-seven, the wound she received thirty years ago still mars her personality. Even though she's now the mother of five children and lives in a lovely home, she gets up at 4:00 A.M. each morning and begins to clean her house! Her children think it's foolish. Her husband can hardly stand it anymore. Her friends rarely come to see her because she doesn't have much time to spend with them.

She has to clean! You see, she doesn't want *anyone* to ever damage her self-esteem again!

There are all too many people whose behavior is motivated by a frantic search to repair a wounded sense of self-esteem. Meet a few of them:

—Charles F., age fifty-two, makes over a hundred thousand dollars a year. He works seventy hours a week and can feel happy about himself only when he is making money. He spends almost no time with his two young children— and hasn't taken a vacation in eight years. As a child, his family was very *poor*.

—Rita N., age twenty-nine, is one of the most promiscuous women in town. She dresses seductively and finds it's very hard to refuse anything to anyone. When she was in high school, she was regarded as being very *unpopular*.

—Craig W., age twenty, is a straight A student in college. He studies almost constantly, and even though he's in his third year of college, he has met only a handful of his classmates. In the first grade, his teacher thought that he was rather *dull*.

Yes, all these people are twisting their lives in exaggerated efforts to heal old wounds to their sense of self-esteem.

When people have a healthy sense of self-esteem, they can take things in their stride. They can

1. bounce back easily from a defeat.
2. meet other people without excessive shyness.
3. risk doing some new things.

4. leave themselves open to novelty and change.
5. feel comfortable in almost any social interaction.
6. try to change their lives in the direction that they want to go.
7. deal with situations in a flexible and sound way.

Most of all, people with a good sense of self-esteem are able to make up their own minds. They listen to others, but when they have to make a decision, they rely on their own inner counsel. They are truly *free!* They are able to alter their concept of themselves to meet changing circumstances, and they usually meet reality head-on.

—Bruce H., age forty, is a case in point. Ten years ago, Bruce was considered one of the boy wonders of Wall Street. Spurred on by the intense public interest in the stock market, he rapidly rose to become the vice president of a small investment house. He helped bring about many mergers, and in the process became a millionaire.

He and his family moved into a large home, and they began to live extravagantly and well. When the glitter and glow began to vanish from stocks a few years later, Bruce's company was badly hurt. Bruce was hurt even worse—because he was financially overextended. As a matter of fact, Bruce was virtually bankrupt!

After a brief period of emotional shock, Bruce wasted little time in blaming himself or others. He devoted all his energies to readjusting his life. He and his wife sold their home and their expensive cars. They dropped their membership in the club. Bruce's wife went back to work.

And with the proceeds from the sale of the house and cars (as well as a loan from a local bank), Bruce opened up a small general store in a rapidly growing suburb. "It's hard work," said Bruce, "but I sleep well at night."

And well he might! A good sense of self-esteem is the best sleeping aid that I know.

❧

Do you know how we get our sense of self-esteem? There are actually a few ways, but the best way is to get it as a *gift* from other people.

As a matter of fact, most of the time our feelings about ourselves are merely the reflected appraisals of others who were close to us.

We get our sense of self-esteem, not because we are told that we should have it, but because we were treated *as if* we were esteemed.

That's very important!

We can't embarrass a child and then expect him or her to grow up with a healthy sense of self-esteem.

Many tribes of American Indians, for example, felt that it was extremely important for their children to grow up with a solid sense of self-esteem.

According to one story, an Indian chief and a missionary sat down for a long talk in order to reconcile their differences. They spoke about many things, and at one point the Indian asked the missionary, "Why don't white folks want their sons to grow up to be braves?"

"Of course, we want our sons to be braves," the missionary replied. "It's very important to white people that our sons become braves!"

"Then how come I once saw a white man slapping his son?" asked the chief. "Every Indian knows that if you don't treat your son with honor, he can never honor himself."

Wise Indian! He knew how to make a brave.

Weed ————————→ People can feel anyway they choose about themselves.

Seed ————————→ Our self-esteem is usually the product of others' esteem for us.

Seed ————————→ A solid sense of self-esteem can be one of our most valuable possessions.

The NN's don't have any time left over to try and help others develop a good sense of self-esteem. They are still working on their own.

The late Eric Berne, a famous psychiatrist and author of the best-selling *Games People Play*, had a good knack for simplifying tough concepts. He knew that every contact between two people resulted in some kind of vibrations in each of them. He knew that when you interact with someone else, both of you are slightly changed as a result of that interaction. Berne called such an interaction a transaction.

Transactions between you and others are called strokes.

You can, in your interaction with others, put them down. Berne called this kind of interactions cold "pricklies."

If you stroke others in a positive way, Berne would say that you gave them a "warm fuzzy."

Warm fuzzies are good for people. They build self-esteem, or they can repair an all-but-shattered self-image.

Warm fuzzies are the bricks that can be used in building a solid personality.

We give warm fuzzies when we

1. tell her that we love her.
2. let him know that he has done a good job.
3. encourage her when she is discouraged.
4. rub his back when he is tired.
5. find something about her that is truly beautiful.
6. send her flowers.
7. remember her birthday.
8. forget his mistake.

We give cold pricklies when we

1. tell her that we once loved someone else.
2. let him know that the job he did wasn't perfect.
3. discourage her from doing something she wants to do.
4. turn away from him when he is tired.
5. find something about her that you can criticize.
6. never give a "just-like-that" gift.
7. forget her birthday.
8. remember his mistakes!

Warm fuzzies are better than cold pricklies in building self-esteem! You know something? *You* can be either a cold pricklie dispenser or a warm fuzzy giver. That's a lot of power to have over the lives and futures of others!

Let's imagine that you died right now. This very moment. What epitaph would they place on your tombstone? Choose either *A* or *B*.

A (your name) was one of the world's greatest cold-pricklies dispensers.

B (your name) was always able to find some warm fuzzies for others.

The planter of the carob tree knew that warm fuzzies were a good investment in someone else's future sense of self-esteem.

Our level of self-esteem is constantly changing. Sometimes we feel good about ourselves, and at other times we don't like ourselves very much at all.

If we try a new task and we master it, our sense of self-esteem rises. It we try a new task and we fail, our sense of self-esteem is likely to fall.

But it's the opinion of others that largely shapes our opinion of ourselves.

A Recent Psychological Experiment

A large group of young women were asked to solve twenty-five short problems. After they did their best, the experimenter looked at the results.

Half the group were told that they did well, and the other half were told that they did poorly (no actual grading was ever done).

After a little while, the experimenter told *all* the subjects the truth. It was all make-believe and their papers were never really graded.

Later on, all the subjects were asked to rank themselves on their ability to solve a problem.

The group that had been told they did poorly weren't able to get over the blow to their sense of self-esteem even though they now knew that the results were phony. They rated themselves rather poorly.

The group that had been told they did well (even though they knew that the results were false) tended to rate themselves rather highly.

We help others find their sense of self-esteem when we let them succeed at a task.

I once observed a wise, old grandfather who waited patiently for many minutes as his five-year-old grandson struggled repeatedly to tie his shoelaces. "Why don't you help him?" asked the child's older brother. "We *both* know how to tie shoelaces," he replied. "And now it's time for Fred to learn how to tie them so that he can also feel good about himself."

It's often hard for us in dealing with those we love to resist the temptation to give unwanted and sometimes unnecessary advice or help.

When we constantly give advice to those around us, we may unwittingly cripple the other person's sense of self-esteem that comes from the ability to come forth with the solution that's really right for him or her. An ancient Chinese proverb proclaims that "there's nothing more blessed on earth than a mother. But there's nothing more blessed in heaven than a mother who knows when to let go the hand!"

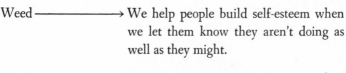

Weed ⟶ We help people build self-esteem when we let them know they aren't doing as well as they might.

Seed ⟶ We help people build self-esteem when we give encouragement.

94

Seed ⟶ We help people build self-esteem when
we let them try things for themselves.

❦

One of the greatest gifts in helping a person's sense of self-esteem is to help that individual bounce back from defeat. Remember the case of Bruce, the stockbroker, and how he pulled his life together? Well, there's something I didn't tell you.

Bruce was married to Claire, and Claire was a very special kind of person. When she saw that Bruce was going through a crisis of self-esteem, she began to give him as much support as he needed.

Each time Bruce's flood of doubt and self-hate was about to overflow his usually strong dam of self-confidence, Claire was there for him with right proportions of sandbagging and support. She

1. reminded Bruce of some of his previous successes.
2. let him know that she would welcome the opportunity to go back to work.
3. showed him that she loved him (even if they weren't going to have a big house or pretty cars).

Without her, Bruce might have gone under. With her, Bruce made it. She was the difference! She was quite a good dispenser of warm fuzzies.

❦

Sometimes, it's tough for people to give the gift of self-esteem to others if they don't feel good about themselves.

95

Several years ago, I worked with a middle-aged woman who was depressed, anxious, and ready for a divorce. I learned from her that her life was made intolerable by a husband who came home from work each day in a carping, critical mood. He was so critical, as a matter of fact, that his children avoided him whenever they possibly could do so.

After he arrived home each day, he would systematically spread gloom from room to room.

"Lisa, I told you to pick up your toys. I nearly killed myself on the steps. Next Christmas, you'll get nothing!"

"John, it's no wonder you're an idiot. You sit there watching old *I Love Lucy* reruns when you have homework to do!"

"Mary, if you don't get off that damned telephone, I'll pull the thing out of the wall."

After listening to this lady, as she catalogued her many dissatisfactions, I understood *why* she wanted a divorce. But I suggested that before she risked throwing out the baby of marriage with the bath water of her dissatisfaction, she might try bringing her husband in for a session. And after much truculent resistance, he finally agreed to come.

For a few minutes, he complained about how awful he felt everyone in the family to be. As he continued to speak without being interrupted, he finally arrived at the painful, hidden agenda that was obscured by the smoke screen of his rage.

"It's hard to help other people feel like winners," he said, "when you feel like such a loser yourself!"

As I listened to him, I learned that his small retail store was in serious difficulty—and the worse the sales figures became—the more critical he became of his family.

After a very short period of time, he made an important decision. He decided that even though he felt like a loser, he didn't have to defeat everyone about him. He realized that even though he was a loser in business, he could become a winner in the business of building self-esteem. And he did!

Weed —————————→ If I feel rotten, I can feel a bit better by dragging everyone down with me.

Seed —————————→ You can sometimes restore your *own* sense of self-esteem by building up rather than tearing down the self-esteem of those who are close to you.

Deed —————————→ When you feel rotten, give some fuzzies instead of pricklies. Then, you won't get hurt by as many thorns.

Try it!

We can help others gain a sense of firm, healthy, self-esteem when we set up realistic standards for them to follow.

It's a little like the story of the youngster who was chewed out by his parents for not doing so well as he should in school.

"It's not that I'm an *under*achiever," replied the boy in defense. "It's that my teacher is an *over*expecter!"

I often work with families in which a child's sense of self-esteem is often sacrificed in the burning fires of parental ambition.

Recently, for example, I saw a girl who was angry, tense, and in danger of becoming a serious problem. She was an excellent pianist and, by the time she was fourteen, she had already given several recitals.

Her parents, spurred on by her success and ability, kept trying to spur her on to new musical heights. They urged her to practice more—and still more. They took her from piano teacher to piano teacher. All had their own theories and exercises and suggestions.

As a result of all the pressure she received, the girl began to doubt her own ability. Soon, she hardly trusted her musical ability at all. Just before her sense of self-esteem was completely shattered, she decided that she would give up music completely.

Seed ──────────→ If people are pushed beyond their ability,
they are likely to give up.

There's a word that isn't used very much among the NN's. And that word is respect. (NN's don't respect anyone, not even themselves.)

Yes, plain, old-fashioned respect can be the magical antidote that can repair a badly damaged sense of self-esteem.

When we respect someone else, we show them we know they are separate, distinct, and unique human beings. We treat them in the same way we would like to be treated.

I recently saw a woman who felt terrible. Although her husband *loved* her a lot, he didn't give her any respect.

He would

1. always suggest that she add a little something more to the stew.
2. recommend what floor wax she should buy.

98

3. suggest to her which necklace she should wear with which dress.
4. tell her whom she should invite to their home.

As a result of his lack of respect for her choices, decisions, feelings, and ideas, her self-esteem was badly damaged.

"You treat me as if I were an idiot," she complained.

"I'm just trying to be helpful," he replied.

She didn't need that kind of help. Instead, she could have used some respect.

People who have a healthy sense of self-esteem know the difference between feelings and actions. They have learned that almost everyone experiences almost every kind of human feeling from time to time. They know that they are not responsible for these feelings, but they are responsible for their actions.

That's a hard lesson to learn!

We gain self-esteem when we say yes to some of our desires and when we say no to others.

We help give our children self-esteem when we help them learn to say no to some of their whims. It takes a lot of consistent, warm discipline before a child can renounce some infantile desires for immediate gratification.

Weed ⟶ We can give our children self-esteem by making sure we gratify all their desires.

Seed ⟶ Children can develop a good sense of self-esteem when they learn how to gain control of their actions.

99

People can begin to feel a sense of self-esteem when they are given some productive work to do. Without work, most people begin to feel restless, and their sense of self-esteem begins to fall.

Have you ever seen the change that often comes over *teenagers* when *they* get a real job? Not a make-work job, but a real job!

As a matter of fact, I'm convinced that part of the reason that adolescence is such a rough time for most families in our country is that most teenagers simply do not have access to a job that could boost their sense of self-esteem.

Even much younger children begin to feel good about themselves when they finish a job.

"Marty, you did a good job in helping me carry in the packages."

"Merry, I'm very proud of how well you cleaned out the closet."

"Judy, the car really gleams since you polished it so well."

"Ellen, your salad was super!"

Yes, doing a good job makes everyone feel good.

Most NN's don't want to expose their children to any problems. They feel that having a problem is somehow a stigma and a visible reminder that they are human. (Besides, having a problem isn't always very pleasurable.)

Sooner or later, however, everyone has problems. It's not *having* the problem—but what we *do* with the problem—that counts!

When we help people close to us solve a problem, we help them grow.

—Leonard S., age thirteen, didn't know whether or not he should continue with his paper route. He took his problem to his dad and wanted a definite answer.

Mr. S. (although he thought he knew the right answer) decided it would be valuable for Leonard to puzzle the problem for a while.

Leonard did—and after much uncertainty came up with a solution that seemed right for him. Mr. S. supported his decision.

I confess that I don't know if Leonard's decision was, indeed, the right one. But, you know—it doesn't matter. What's important is that Mr. S. supported Leonard's decision, and because he did, Leonard began to grow!

Some Additional Seeds

1. Problem-solving is part and parcel of being a person.
2. We give people the gift of self-esteem when we let them know that *everyone* has problems.
3. Self-esteem grows when we help others look at their assets and not just their liabilities.
4. We can help people's self-esteem when we encourage them to be assertive.
5. Did you know that a big component of self-esteem is self-forgiveness?
6. No one (no, no one at all!) can ever change everything all at once! Our problems are solved in gradual stages!
7. Most people who have self-esteem problems really have overevaluated esteem of others.
8. Some people try to inflate their own sagging sense of self-esteem by deflating the sense of self-esteem of others!

9. Most formal manners represent society's way of helping others maintain their own sense of self-esteem.

Self-esteem—what a wonderful gift to give to those you love! P.S. Don't ever compare Charles with Pete or Alice with Margaret. It will ruin their sense of self-esteem.

Yes, it will.

8. The Gift of Giving Up a Bad Habit

Sow an Act, and you reap a Habit;
Sow a Habit, and you reap a Character;
Sow a Character, and you reap a Destiny.

—ANONYMOUS

"YOU CAN ACTIVELY SEEK disapproval and work on yourself to not be upset. Select someone who is bound to disagree and, flying in the face of the disapproval, maintain your position calmly. You'll get better at not being upset and not having to alter your own views," writes Wayne W. Dyer in *Your Erroneous Zones.*

Among the NN's, altering a piece of one's behavior to suit someone *else* is one of the cardinal sins.

—If your radio is on very loud and *they* don't like it, let *them* go away.
—If you have something to say to your friend in the theater while a performance is taking place, let *them* get another seat.
—If you want to smoke your cigar in the plane, let *them* take another flight.

The nerve of some people who want *you* to change an annoying or unpleasant habit so that things will also be more comfortable for them! Who needs *them,* when there's *me!*

🌷

When people care for and love each other, they not only are concerned with their own welfare and happiness, they are also concerned about the welfare and happiness of those close to them. Closeness almost always brings friction.

More often, I have found the solution to this friction in the soothing balm of compromise and a willingness to change certain annoying aspects of ourselves.

Do you know what we call a relationship where there's *as much* concern with someone's else's needs as there is with your own?

We call it love! Yes, it's love when you strike that vital balance between your own needs and the needs of your partner.

Sometimes compromise is easy, and one doesn't need the wisdom of Solomon to make the decision. Plain common sense will do just fine.

Phil and Amy are a case in point. Phil is a tennis nut, and Amy is a ski bunny. If Phil had his way, he would spend their winter vacation on a tropical island, where he could play tennis from early morning until his sneakers would wear out. If Amy had her way, she would spend that week on the highest slope in Colorado, where she could ski from the time the lift starts to run until the snow melts. The solution? One year they go to the islands and the next to the slopes. During the rest of the season, Amy spends a day skiing with her friends, and Phil plays some tennis with his group. A lot of the time, they work out the details together.

❦

Sometimes the solution is not so simple, and a habit that one person has may affect the health or happiness of the other, as well as the individual's!

—John R., age thirty-seven, has been drinking too much. Twice on the way home from dinner parties, he has had bad accidents. The last time he nearly killed not only himself but his wife as well.

John's drinking habit puts his wife in danger!

—Virginia S., age thirty-four, finds it hard to resist impulse spending. As soon as she sees something she likes, she buys it. As a result of her constant spending, she and her husband have been unable to save enough for a down payment on a house.

Virginia's spending habit frustrates her husband's desire for a home!

—Ralph V., age twenty-eight, has been divorced for two years. He's scheduled to call his daughter every Wednesday night, and he's supposed to visit her every Saturday. Sometimes he gets involved with other things, and so his daughter never gets called, or a hoped-for visit is cancelled.

Ralph's forgetfulness habit does not allow his daughter to develop a healthy image of men.

If you could change an unhealthy or an unhappy habit of yours, what a wonderful gift that would be not only for you but also for those you love.

❦

If you would like to change a habit, I'll tell you how to do it.

In recent years, psychologists have learned more about habits than ever before. Psychological journals are filled with new techniques and ideas for changing habits. Interestingly enough, habit change is not so terribly complicated, and most plans for changing habits boil down to a few helpful techniques.

If there's a habit you would like to change, read on. If not, why don't you skip the rest of this chapter?

Weed ⟶ I'm me! Anyone who wants me to change anything about myself is intruding on my space.

Seed ⟶ Most of the things you do affect other people as well as yourself.

The most important thing to remember about habits is that they are learned. As a matter of fact, psychologists define a habit as being a "learned, fixed way of gratifying a need."

All healthy human beings, for example, have a need to eat. It's by eating that we can nourish ourselves. We all need food—but the foods we like to eat are the foods that we learned to eat.

If you grew up in the United States, chances are that you learned to like meat. You learned to like meat because when you were young and hungry, your parents gave you a hamburger. It satisfied your hunger, so you got to like it. It all seems very natural for someone to like meat!

But if you grew up in Japan, chances are that you learned to like raw fish. You learned to like raw fish because when you were young and hungry, you were given some raw fish. It satisfied your hunger, so you got to like it, and it seems very natural to do so.

That's how you came to

1. eat liver.
2. hate tongue.
3. eat onions.

Can you imagine how brave the first person to eat a lobster must have been? Can you imagine how much courage it took to get past all those legs and shells and stuff to get to the meat?

Do you remember when you learned to like lobster? (Some people never get past the legs and shells and stuff.)

Sometimes, it's tough to learn a habit. Let's take smoking for example! Most people begin to choke and cough when they start to smoke. They have to really work at it for a long time until their lungs will tolerate a blast of hot gases and smoke without coughing. But they keep at it because they want to learn how to smoke. When you're a teenager, smoking seems to be cool and tough and very grown-up. So if you want to be cool and tough and grown-up, you better learn to smoke. And if you work hard enough at it, you can learn! You see, you can learn *bad* habits in the same manner that you learn good habits.

Weed ─────────→ We are born liking things because of instinct.

Seed ─────────→ Most of the things we like are *learned.*

❦

Now here's something that may surprise you! ANYTHING THAT HAS BEEN LEARNED CAN BE UNLEARNED.

But, it takes a lot of motivation and desire. And I mean a *lot* of motivation.

In my work with people who want to change habits, I find that the most important factor in a successful outcome is the degree of the desire to change.

A great many people who think they want to change really *don't* want to change. They like things just the way they are, and they don't want to invest the time and care and discomfort that go into changing a habit.

A while ago, a man I was working with said that he wanted to stop smoking. I asked him about his smoking, and he said he had tried to give up cigarettes in the past, but that he "simply couldn't give them up." I then asked him, "Suppose I told you that if you didn't give up cigarettes for a week, your wife and your four children would be guillotined on Monday morning. Could you give up smoking for a week?" "Of course I could!" he replied.

You see, most people *can* give up a habit if the stakes are high enough! I've learned that when people say that they *can't* give up a habit, they are, in fact, saying they *won't* give up the habit.

The first step in giving up a habit is to increase your motivation to do so. Sometimes that requires an understanding of some of the payoffs you unconsciously get for keeping the habit going.

One woman, for example, wanted to change her habit of overspending. She resolved to do so, but couldn't succeed until she realized that by her spending she was punishing her husband. That was a big payoff, because she was very angry at him.

When she learned to deal with her anger in a more direct and a healthier way, she found she was able to alter her spending habit.

Sometimes, resistance to changing a habit is not complicated, and it can be overcome by increasing our motivation to do so. Here are some of the things you can do.

1. Make a list of all the reasons why you should change the habit.
2. Make a list of all the things your habit does for you. Are there any other ways you can get the same results?
3. Up the ante for giving up the habit. (One girl promised herself a trip to Bermuda when she lost twenty pounds.)
4. *Make* the decision. Really make the decision to give it up!

Weed ⟶ Long-term habits are impossible to change.

Seed ⟶ A habit can be changed if there is enough motivation and understanding.

❦

A hint about changing habits! Don't be too general. You have to be *specific* about the behaviors you want to change.

You'll find it hard to do something with, "I'd like to be a better person." It's easier to do something with, "I'd like to lose my temper less often."

The second step in changing a habit (if you have decided you're going to do it) is to keep a *list*. Yes! A plain old list can help you change a habit.

On your list, you should note each instance of the behavior you want to change. If, for example, you want to lose fifty pounds, it's important to list everything you eat. So your list might look like this:

Saturday, April 8

  8:05 A.M. six ounces of orange juice
          three slices of bacon
          two small eggs (boiled)
          cup of coffee with artificial sweetener
10:07 A.M. cup of coffee with sweetener
11:12 A.M. two sticks of chewing gum

                                    etc.
          Yes, list everything—even the gum!

It's only recently that psychologists have learned how important it is to keep an accurate record of a habit, but Benjamin Franklin knew it two hundred years ago.

When Franklin wanted to change his behavior so that he would improve in areas of "Sincerity" and "Industry," he got a little book in which he kept a day-by-day account of his behavior.

As Franklin noted his errors in his diary, he was surprised to find that he was (in his words) "so much fuller of faults" than he ever thought he would be.

His reaction was not unlike that of a man who, in keeping a food diary, commented to me, "It's astounding how much I put into my mouth during that past week. No wonder I'm so fat."

After the diary has been kept a while, it's time to sit down and take a long, hard look at what's happening! You have to put on your detective hat; get out your magnifying glass and figure out what are the triggers (cues) that set off the chain of behavior.

A patient of mine, for example, who was working hard on overcoming a heavy smoking habit, found that his smoking behavior was triggered by a variety of events that caused him to reach into his pocket, take out a cigarette, and begin to smoke.

He noted that some of the triggers were

1. getting up in the morning.
2. drinking a cup of coffee.
3. getting a phone call.
4. making a phone call.
5. seeing the *end* of a television program.

In looking over his list, he was surprised to discover—as many others do—how automatic his smoking behavior had become.

Studies of people who develop habits reveal that, for a complex variety of reasons, they tend to respond to a trigger somewhat differently from a person who is not likely to get snared on the "hook of a habit."

Studies of people who tend to overeat, for example, show that these people tend to eat *because food is there*. People who do not develop weight problems are more likely to eat *because they are hungry*.

It's strange, but that's the way it is! Heavy people have learned to eat when they see food, whereas people who don't have problems with their weight are likely to eat only when they get hungry.

Seed ⟶ When you can find the triggers that set off a piece of behavior, you have made an important step in overcoming that behavior.

❧

Now that you have found the triggers, you can learn the magic word that can cure a bad habit. That's the word SUBSTITUTE! In my work with people, I find that there are only a few people who can give up something successfully for a long period of time.

Some people can give up smoking by going cold turkey, and they stop once and for all—all at once. Most of the people who do this, by the way, do so when they become supermotivated, usually by a real scare. One patient of mine, for example, was sitting at his desk smoking a cigarette when he felt sharp chest pains! His secretary drove him to the hospital, and a rather serious heart attack was diagnosed. That was five years ago, and since that time he has not had another cigarette.

Most people, however, don't like to give up anything. They feel as if something is being taken away from them.

Therefore, in working with people who have to give up a bad habit, I try to help them think of what habit they will take up —rather than give up! It sounds a little nutty, but it works.

So the next time you want to give up something, figure out what you'll take up instead!

With people who want to give up smoking, for example, I find that there are certain helpful habits they can take up instead. Some of the habits I suggest they take up (substitute) when the trigger for the old smoking habit gets cocked are

1. sipping ice water.
2. popping peppermint lifesavers.
3. pushing their big toes into the side of their shoes while they count to ten.
4. closing their eyes and thinking of resting on a tropical beach.

When you substitute a new habit that you just took up, you find that the old habit gradually disappears. As the trigger situation passes, so does the desire for the old habit.

Weed ⟶ With a little willpower, you can give up any habit.

Seed ⟶ It's best to adopt a new habit that will replace the old one.

❧

Here's a good habit you should take up. It's called RELAXATION!

"I'm wound up as tight as a drum. If I could only relax, I would be O.K."
"I'm so jealous of people who are relaxed."
"I went to the doctor today, and he told me that I need to relax. I wish I knew how."

You can learn to relax! Relaxation is a habit, and with some proper training you can produce a state of relaxation in yourself whenever you want.

It's best to start learning relaxation by sitting alone in a quiet room. Close your eyes.

Now clench your right fist as hard as you can. More! Still more! O.K.—let's go! Still more!

Picture your hand as being an empty sack, and all the tension is running out of your fingers like sand. Still more! Let it all flow out.

Now do the same exercise with your left hand. O.K. Now work with every part of your body in turn—chest, neck, back, thighs—all of you.

Pay particular attention to your breathing. Let your breathing come naturally, but each time you exhale, try to imagine you are expelling tension. Each time you inhale, think of yourself as filling up with relaxation.

If you practice the above exercise for twenty-minute periods a day, you'll probably be better able to relax at will in a short period of time. All you will have to do then is to tell yourself to relax—and you know what? You will!

It works as well as meditation or yoga. (And, besides, you don't have to bring fruit and flowers to your guru.)

Weed ——————————→ I can't relax. I'm always tense.

Seed ——————————→ Relaxation can be learned.

Deed ——————————→ Practice relaxation twice a day.

Here's another good habit you should take up. It's called EXERCISE.

In my work with people who want to give up bad habits, I find that very few of them understand how helpful exercise can be. Exercise is an ideal substitute habit for the one that you want to give up.

One man, for example, wanted to cut down on his drinking. He usually would come home—drained and exhausted—and then would pour himself three fingers of Scotch. After fifteen minutes or so, he started to feel less fatigued and more relaxed.

He decided to take a jog instead of a drink—and he was amazed to find that, after a half hour of exercise, he began to feel less fatigued and more relaxed. After a shower, he felt fine. His alcohol consumption began to fall!

Jogging is fine, but it may be too strenuous for you. If it is, a brisk walk or some simple isometric exercise will do.

Weed ⟶ Exercise is good only for the young.

Seed ⟶ Exercise can be a valuable tool when you're trying to learn to change a habit.

❦

A word or two about getting rid of a nasty or troubling phobia.

Most people who have a phobia suffer a lot from their fears. The reasons why a phobia begins can sometimes be complicated. At times, phobias represent convenient hooks upon which we can hang our anxieties. At other times, a phobia will develop during a period of depression.

A problem can often symbolically represent a conflict that's going on within us—that we find hard to deal with directly. Sometimes, it's just the result of faulty learning!

Regardless of why a phobia began, however, it usually becomes a habit. And sometimes the habit remains long after the conflict has passed.

Mary F., age twenty-nine, had a lot of marital troubles two years ago. She was depressed and frightened and had the thought that she would like to pack her clothes, get into her car, and take off with a man at the office.

During this period of time, she developed a marked fear of driving her car! As a matter of fact, she got so scared that she couldn't drive her car unless her husband was with her.

Mary and her husband gradually resolved their marital problems, but, in spite of the fact that they were now happy, her phobia remained to plague her. She had *learned* to become afraid of driving alone!

In the past few years, a lot of research has been done on phobias—and the results of *all* the studies agree! (Isn't that nice

—in the complicated world of psychological research—to have *all* of the studies agree?)

The key to getting over a phobia is exposure to the thing that you fear!

Yes! If you are afraid of something and you do it, you'll get rid of your fear. If you just sit around thinking about it, you will just get more scared.

Old Doctor Freud knew that, and all the present research indicates he was right on target!

- —If you're scared of dogs—and you want to get rid of your fear—get a puppy.
- —If you are afraid of the subway, take a short ride on one.
- —If you're frightened of close spaces, go sit in a small room for a few minutes.

You might initially feel uncomfortable, but if you stare your fear directly in the eye (if you can fortify yourself with relaxation exercises), your fear will usually back down.

Weed ⟶ I think I'll wait until I know *why* I'm afraid. Then maybe I won't be afraid anymore.

Seed ⟶ If I do what I'm afraid of, I won't be so afraid.

❧

If you can give up a bad habit by yourself, that's fine! But if you would like some help, there's more available than ever before.

People who band together in a group to work on a common

problem often can help each other beat a bad habit. In recent years, self-help groups have begun to spring up like mushrooms after a rain.

In almost every part of the country, for example, groups have been started by the American Cancer Society that can help you give up smoking!

Some of the other groups that can be of help are

1. Alcoholics Anonymous.
2. Overeaters Anonymous.
3. Recovery, Inc.

Breaking a habit can be a lonely job, and you don't have to do it alone!

❦

A Little Story

A couple of years ago, I was working with the wife of a local businessman. She was scared to death of flying. She had *never* flown before, but she was sure that if she ever got into a plane she would panic.

Her husband was longing to travel, but because of her fear of flying, their travels were limited.

One day, she read about an airline that was running an experimental program, conducted by a psychologist, that was designed to help people fly without fear.

"What a wonderful gift it would be for my husband," she said, "if I could begin to fly."

And it was! (She enjoyed it, too!)

Some Additional Seeds

1. Habits aren't broken immediately—it takes a little time.
2. Remember, anything that has been learned can be unlearned.
3. Contrary to NN propaganda, you're not less of a person if you change some part of yourself to please others. (People used to call it being civilized.)
4. Sometimes, the best way to change people's reaction to us is to change ourselves.
5. *Everyone* has problems in some area of self-control. If you try your best, that's the important thing.
6. Change doesn't always hurt.
7. Knowing that you are the victim of circumstances is only the first part. The most important thing is to learn how to play the hand that life dealt you.
8. The longest and most difficult journey *always* has been to begin with a first step.
9. You could start right now!

9. The Gift of Self-Disclosure

"Love *is* self-disclosure."

—SIDNEY JOURARD

DID YOU EVER HEAR the one about the boy who never talked?

It seems that there was this boy who was normal in every respect. Only he never talked to anyone! His concerned parents took him to psychologists and to psychiatrists. They took him to throat specialists and to speech therapists. Still, he didn't talk.

One day, when he was about sixteen years old, he looked up from the breakfast table and said to his mother, "The oatmeal is cold!"

His mother was astounded to hear her son communicate. After she recovered from the shock of having him speak for the first time, she eagerly replied, "John, you *can* talk. Why, oh, why, haven't you ever said anything before?"

"Because before this," he replied, "everything was always O.K."

It's a funny story, but it's not so funny in real life when people closely interact with others without disclosing their feelings and needs to those they love.

Most relationships either grow and expand, or they become stale and decline. Self-disclosure—letting someone else discover more about you—can turn a wilting relationship into a flourishing one. It can also help sustain an already healthy friendship or marriage. Bottling up feelings, resentments, and hopes is unhealthy; it also deprives others of really knowing who you are.

Playing it cool is a current American game. It's based on the mistaken notion that if *others* know something about you, they will use that knowledge to hurt or harm you.

Playing it cool is fine when you're playing bridge or poker—and the card player who can keep a poker face can often be the big winner. In human relationships, however, poker-faced, nondisclosing people are the big losers.

When you don't let it out, there's no space for anyone to come in.

(NN's aren't interested in disclosing themselves to others. They don't want to let others learn anything meaningful about themselves. They only want to tell people those flamboyant or dramatic things about themselves that would tend to place them in a positive light!)

Weed ⟶ It's best not to let others know too much about you.

Seed ⟶ When I genuinely communicate my feelings and ideas to someone, I am truly giving a gift of myself.

❦

To give the gift of self-disclosure to others is not as easy as it might seem. There are many hurdles that we have to jump over before we can disclose ourselves to other people.

Hurdles

1. Big Boys Don't Cry

   It's often tougher for men to express their feelings openly because to do so doesn't seem to be macho. Indeed, inexpressiveness is an almost national "disease" that has been caught by many American men.

—David V., age thirty-six, owned a successful printing shop for many years. One day, a new print shop opened up a block away. Many of David's old customers were lured to this new shop by lower prices, and soon David found that his profits began to decline. He felt awful about the competition, and he began to feel frightened about his ability to successfully meet this new threat.

   He would often return home from work glum, withdrawn, and quiet. Elaine, his wife, wanted to know what the problem was. David found it hard to disclose to her that he was scared. So he didn't say much at all! Elaine, not knowing what the silence was all about, thought that David must be seeing another woman.

   Because of his inability to disclose, David now had two problems instead of just one.

2. It's Shameful Not to Be Like the Books Tell You You Should Be

—Suzy R., age twenty-eight, has been married for two years. Since her marriage, she has been deeply troubled because she finds she has been unable to achieve orgasm. She is so ashamed about not living up to her notions about what Bob expects her to be like that she *pretends* to be sexually gratified.

Not knowing that she's not, Bob does not vary his love-machine techniques. And he blames Suzy's bouts of painful depression on her job.

3. If You Can't Say Something Nice, Don't Say Anything At All

—Wilma J., age thirty-two, is team-teaching a sixth-grade class with Linda R. Both are supposed to have equal responsibility for the class—and, indeed, that's the way things were for the first two months of the year!

Gradually, however, Linda began to do less work and Wilma, not wanting to make waves, began to pull Linda's share of the load as well as her own.

The harder Wilma worked, the less Linda had to do. Linda had no awareness of how resentful and unhappy Wilma was becoming. She saw Wilma as an eager beaver and kept telling everyone how lucky she was to be working with such a capable person.

When Wilma developed an ulcer, her doctor told her that he was less concerned with what she ate than he was with what was eating her.

Yes, self-disclosure is not always so easy.

Weed ——————→ Silent types are usually strong.

Weed ——————→ If you tell others how you feel, they'll see you as a complainer.

Weed ——————→ If you let problems go by without doing anything about them, things will get better by themselves.

Seed ——————→ Self-disclosure can prevent and resolve misunderstandings between people.

❦

If we can't be honest with others, we can't ever be honest with ourselves. And when we aren't honest with ourselves, we become unauthentic.

Unauthentic people soon become robotlike. It's almost as if they were made out of plastic rather than of real flesh and blood.

Plastic, unauthentic people tend to live plastic, unauthentic lives.

Plastic People

1. Have become so used to saying what other people want to *hear* that they soon have hardly anything to say at all.
2. Have become so used to not disclosing their feelings that they soon act as if they didn't have any feelings at all.
3. Have become so used to saying the *right* thing that they sometimes say it at the *wrong* time.

Most healthy people prefer to interact with a *real* person rather than with a *plastic* imitation.

In our fast-moving, easy-solution, prepackaged culture, a lot of us are in constant danger of turning into plastic.

I used to have lunch sometimes in a quick-food restaurant that served pretty good roast beef sandwiches. The only problem was that all the girls in this restaurant used to dress in the same way, and they were all trained to say "Howdy, Partner" when they took your order.

A simple "Hello" would have been much better; the "Howdy-Partner" greeting was as plastic as the teaspoons. I don't eat there anymore!

One of the best preventatives you can use to ward off the possibility of catching a case of creeping plasticity is to remain authentic. And you can remain authentic only when you disclose your feelings, your hopes, your desires, and your resentments.

And if you can remain authentic, you can then give those around you some wonderful gifts.

You are able to give

1. A truly honest opinion
2. A spontaneous reaction
3. A shared hope
4. An instantaneous response.

Remember the story of Pinocchio? That poor little guy remained a dumb block of wood until he began to feel and share feelings. Then he became a person!

Seed ⟶ We have much more to give to others when we remain authentic.

Seed ⟶ One of the best ways to remain authentic is to disclose our true feelings to other people.

Healthy people have the capacity to conceal parts of themselves from others. Each time we conceal something from someone who is close to us, however, the relationship becomes a little poorer.

If we conceal too much, the relationship gets very poor, indeed. If the relationship gets too poor, it usually becomes bankrupt. And that's the end of that relationship!

❦

I heard a very sad story a couple of years ago. A man who was married to a lovely woman for thirty-seven years came home from work only to find that his wife had suffered a massive stroke that day. She was rushed to the hospital, but in spite of the best available medical attention, died a few hours later.

After the funeral this man, in shock and grief, told his best friend, "You know what's the worst thing of all? I loved her more than anyone in this whole world, and I was never able to tell her. I was never one to talk about my feelings a lot."

In recent years, thousands of couples recognizing the importance of self-disclosure and open communication have attended marriage encounter weekends.

This highly successful movement, in which couples learn to communicate with each other, was founded in Spain by a Spanish priest, Father Gabriel Calvo, who was concerned by the large number of people who consulted him because of dissatisfaction and unhappiness with their marriages.

At the core of the marriage encounter experience is a process called dialogue. During a dialogue, couples are encouraged to exchange feelings and to disclose their reactions to each other.

It's not unusual for couples who attend a marriage encounter to come home feeling that they have experienced the most wonderful weekend of their lives. For the first time, many people begin to experience the sense of tremendous joy that can come from self-disclosure and open communication.

One patient, after attending a marriage encounter meeting told me, "It was incredible to be able to spend a weekend revealing how I truly felt. What a wonderful luxury it was to say what I wanted to say. I don't think I've ever been happier."

Weed ⟶ When we tell someone that we love them, we either want something from them, or else we're just acting like teenagers.

Seed ⟶ It's important to be able to tell loved ones that we love them.

❧

It's terribly important to disclose our interests and our needs to those that we love in a *clear and definite* way.

Typical Dialogue in a Poor Marriage

He: "I don't know what happened. I came home and I sat down to watch the evening news, and when I came into the dining room to eat supper, she wasn't talking to me. I can't understand it!"

Me: "What did your husband do that bothered you so much?"

She: "He *should* know!"

He: "I *don't* know!"

She: "Well, you *should* know!"

He: "I don't know!"

She: "See what I mean, he's not interested."

Me: "How can *he* know if *you* don't tell him?"

He: "Why don't you tell me what's the matter?"

She: "You *should* know!"

126

It's always incredible to me to find the large number of people who hold others responsible for actions that could be changed if only the "injured" persons would disclose what their needs were in a particular situation that caused them to become unhappy.

It's important to *tell*. It's important to *talk*. No one is a mind reader!

I once worked with a couple whose marriage was in serious trouble. It was so troubled that the husband decided he wanted a divorce.

He complained about a lot of things, but one complaint was curious. He said that during the past five years, he spent every Sunday having dinner at his mother-in-law's home, when he would rather have been at home watching the football game.

"Why didn't you tell your wife that you wanted to stay home on Sunday and watch the football game?" I asked.

"Well," he replied, "the kids always enjoy visiting with my in-laws, and I wanted them to enjoy themselves."

Weed ——————→ If a person truly loves us, he or she will know what *we* want without asking.

Seed ——————→ We can never accuse people of turning us down unless we tell them what we want.

Seed ——————→ Clear self-disclosure is the best kind.

It's outrageous how often it happens. The man who visited his mother-in-law all of the time and never disclosed to his wife what he truly wanted was like:

1. the woman who went to the movies every Sunday night. She hated going to the movies every Sunday, but she

thought her husband would like to go each week. Because *she* didn't say anything, *he* thought that *she* wanted to go, so *he* kept taking her.

2. the man who ate fish cakes every Friday night. *He* hated eating fish cakes every Friday night, but he thought that his wife loved fish cakes. *She* wasn't all that crazy about fish cakes, but since her husband ate so many of them, *she* thought that *he* liked them, so *she* kept making fish cakes.

3. the child who learned from his classmates that there wasn't a *real* Santa Claus. *He* didn't want to disappoint his parents by letting *them* know that there wasn't a real Santa Claus. In order to please them, *he* kept making believe that *he* believed in Santa. *His* parents, in order to please *him*, kept talking about Santa Claus even though it would have been much easier for *them* to simply get *his* Christmas list and buy him what *he* wanted.

Seed ⟶ Open self-disclosure can be the gift that can solve many difficult and touchy situations.

❧

It's hard enough to disclose feelings of love and warmth. It's even harder to disclose negative or critical feelings to those we love.

When you want to disclose negative feelings to someone you love, you know you're on the right track when you can feel confident that the disclosures you're about to make are really designed to *help* the situation and not to *hurt* the other person.

It's been said that the art of diplomacy truly consists of saying and doing unpleasant things in the nicest possible way.

Some NN's I know conceal their attacks and hatred of others by claiming that they are merely self-disclosing!

Weed ⟶ You should say *whatever* you want to say, *however* you want to say it.

Seed ⟶ Self-disclosure is important, but it's *also* important to reveal ourselves to others in a way that won't leave them emotionally destroyed.

One of the most helpful hints in dealing with a problem you have with another person is to remember not to attack the *person*. It's best if you merely say how *you* feel about a particular situation.

One man, for example, was furious with his wife because of the way she used and abused the telephone. His wife had a bad case of chronic telephonitis, and, from early in the morning until late at night, she was either making or receiving telephone calls.

He became particularly enraged at dinner time. Often he would be just about to talk to his wife about something when the phone would ring, and he would then try and choke down his dinner while his wife ate hers with a telephone receiver cradled on her neck.

The unhappy telephone situation continued for a long period of time until he could hardly stand it any longer. Finally, he blurted out, "I can't take it anymore. You're a telephone freak, and I'm tired of it."

As could be predicted, the next effect of this attack was to make his wife defensive and, as a result, she used the telephone even more than ever.

Like most people who feel attacked, she

1. felt defensive.
2. felt that she had to justify her actions.
3. became more defiant.
4. became resistant and hostile.
5. tried to show she was really right.

After a brief (but it felt as if it were forever) period of guerilla warfare, this man tried another (and wiser) approach.

He leveled with his wife and he told her not what *she* was, but what *he* desired.

He told her that

1. *he* looked forward to talking with *her* at the end of a day.
2. *he* found it hard to enjoy eating when he kept getting interrupted by telephone calls.
3. *he* enjoyed her company and resented sharing it with others during dinner.

As a result of his open and frank self-disclosure with his wife, she took a long, hard look at the telephone situation.

A couple of days later, when he came home, he found that she had spoken to the telephone company and had had a little device installed on their telephone. Now, during dinner, she turns the ring of the phone off so that dinner can proceed without annoying distractions. After dinner is finished, she turns on the phone.

Weed ⎯⎯⎯⎯⎯⎯→ If you're going to be honest, *you* better tell others what *they* should do.

Seed ⎯⎯⎯⎯⎯⎯→ You'll have a better chance of getting your message across to other people if you *don't* attack *them* but merely tell *them* what *you* feel.

❧

One of the most helpful things we can do to help open channels of communication is to let the person we are with know the state of our mood.

Everyone has moods. Yes, everyone has highs and lows. In recent years, psychologists have learned that the fluctuation of human moods is as normal as the variation in the tides of the ocean.

In my work with people, I've learned that it's important (particularly if we are feeling very high or very low) to let those we love know where we are at.

It doesn't have to be an exact barometric reading, but some indication is important.

Such a reading can help the other person understand when to avoid sensitive topics, and what your predictable response is likely to be.

One couple I know get along extraordinarily well. They rarely have bitter fights, and periods of normal disagreements between them are usually short and are usually resolved quickly.

When I asked them to tell me the secret of their compatibility, the wife replied, "You know I found out a long time ago that we were both moody people. We used to fight a lot, and most of our fights were over nothing at all. It was mostly the mood we were in. I realized one day, after a day at the zoo, that even the rattlesnakes give some warning to people before they strike! If rattlesnakes could do it, why can't people?

"Since that time, if either of us is in a *terrible* mood, we let the other one know where we're at. Believe me, in the long run, it helps a lot! The other night, for example, Jack came home from the office and told me he was in a real rotten mood, so I knew it *wasn't* time to tell him that the electric company had come and had told me that. . . ."

Wise Woman!

Weed ──────────→ "If you have something to say, say it! It's foolish to worry about someone else's moods."

Seed ──────────→ When we self-disclose to others, it's also important to let them know what kind of mood we are in. *Showing* them isn't enough; we also have to *tell* them.

❦

There's some evidence to show that kids grow up to be disturbed and unhappy if we give them double-bind messages.

A double-bind message is a communication that says one thing but means another. A classic double-bind message is something such as, "Go away—closer," or "I've been worried about how much you've been smoking. You're really too young to smoke. Here! You can have one of mine."

One family I'm working with has a son who is severely disturbed. This boy is almost always getting into trouble in school.

Most of the time, he gets into trouble because he becomes overly aggressive with his teachers.

A few weeks ago, the family came in to see me, and the father reported a particularly cruel incident in which his son humiliated his teacher. As he told the story in front of his son, he said that he was very angry! But he was smirking! You see, his son was expressing some of his father's own, old, unresolved feelings of rebelliousness toward authority.

So when we talk to children, it's particularly important that we

1. send a very straight message.
2. make sure we tell them what *we* feel without telling them what *they* feel.

   ("You always take the easy way out" isn't as helpful as "I'm really concerned about the poor grades that were sent to me by the school.")
3. watch out we don't put them down!
4. use words that *they* understand.

   (The meaning of words can change quickly! A few years ago, the word *tough* meant hard; now *tough* means the same as *super* or *cool*.)

Yes! Disclosures to children are particularly important.

❦

Do you know that research shows that people who make self-disclosures are more likely to receive self-disclosures in return?

Are you wondering why people haven't given you the gift of some of their *real* feelings?

WHAT KIND OF SELF-DISCLOSURE HAVE YOU GIVEN THEM?

Some Additional Seeds

1. The healing and helping in psychotherapy is based upon the ability of someone to disclose.
2. People who are open usually have more friends than people who are unwilling to disclose themselves to others.
3. If you're the first person to risk saying "Hello" to someone else, you're unlikely to have the other person say "Good-bye" to you.
4. Why don't you try to risk a period of letting go of some of the secrets that you always felt could never be disclosed to anyone else?
5. *Never*—but *never*— let someone else think you're making a self-disclosure when you really are telling them what they want to hear.
6. It's good to guard someone else's self-disclosures as zealously as if they were your own.
7. Playing it cool is a good game for penguins! *People* are better off in an atmosphere of warm communication and frequent self-disclosure.

10. The Gift of Helping Someone Learn Something New

Man is the only one that knows nothing, that can learn nothing without being taught. He can neither speak nor walk nor eat and, in short he can do nothing at the prompting of nature only, but weep.

—PLINY THE ELDER, *Natural History, Book VII*

Once upon a time, there was a little boy by the name of Albert. Albert was a happy, healthy boy who enjoyed new experiences.

One day, Albert was given a gentle, laboratory white rat to play with. Albert showed no fear of the rat, and he seemed to enjoy his contacts with his new furry friend.

As part of an experiment, a loud noise was sounded the next time Albert was given the rat to play with. After a few experiences of his hearing that terrible sound—just at the time that he was given the white rat—Albert's behavior began to change. He now reacted with fear whenever he saw the animal. He also started to act fearful when he saw other small animals as well.

Albert had *learned* to be afraid!

It would have been better had he *learned* something that could have enriched his life!

Consider

1. Compared to a gorilla, humans are *weaker*.
2. Compared to an antelope, humans are *slower*.
3. Compared to a bird, humans are *clumsier*.

Compared to all the other species of animals, however, humans are *smarter!* They're smarter because they have a great capacity for *learning!* Indeed, one could say that the most genuinely human characteristic is this great capacity to continue to learn.

The behavior of most other species is controlled mostly by *instinct*. A human's behavior is controlled mostly by *learning*.

You learned

1. to read.
2. to speak English.
3. to cook.
4. to eat with a fork.
5. to swim.
6. to ice-skate.
7. to ride a bike.

You learned those things and many others. As a matter of fact, you probably don't even remember *learning* everything that you know and do. You've known most things so long that it seems as if you were born knowing them.

People who live rich, gratifying, and happy lives are usually people who have learned a lot of skills. They also have learned how to enjoy using these skills with other people. They remain interested in learning!

Indeed, if there is one outstanding characteristic of emotionally healthy people, I would venture to say it's their desire to continue to learn and to grow. They try to continue to master new things during their entire life span.

There used to be a lot of nonsense around about how difficult it was for older people to learn new skills. Today, most psychologists know that the idea that "old dogs can't learn new tricks" is rubbish. *Anyone,* in good physical health, can continue to learn. Those who stop learning (even if they are twenty-five years old) become old.

I once knew a patient who, at age twenty-three, was very *old.* Although she was an efficient legal secretary, she had very few skills outside of her job.

As a child, she was raised in a strict, unhappy home where there was little or no intellectual curiosity that could spark her interest. Although she was a good student in school, her parents viewed extracurricular activities as a waste of time and effort.

When she was graduated from secretarial school, she found a good job. Because she was a hard worker, she advanced more rapidly and soon made enough money to move into her own apartment.

She was terribly lonely, however, for she had few skills that could help her build bridges to other people.

She realized how *empty* her life was while on a vacation cruise.

On the ship they

1. had a swimming pool, but she didn't know how to swim!
2. had a bridge tournament, but she didn't know how to play bridge!
3. had dancing every night, but she had never learned how to dance!
4. had gourmet meals, but she had never learned to like good cuisine!

When she came back from the cruise, she was miserable—utterly miserable—and she decided to come for some therapy.

After a few sessions, it was quite clear that much of her barren life was simply due to the fact that she never had learned any of the social skills that would help her relate to other people.

With much initial trepidation and hesitation, she began taking some dancing lessons. She liked them so much that she started to take some cooking lessons.

You know what happened? The more she learned, the less depressed she became!

Weed ⟶ If you're lucky, you learn a lot of skills when you're young. If you didn't, it's almost *impossible* to learn new things when you're older.

Seed ⟶ A person can learn new skills throughout an entire lifetime.

Seed ⟶ An emotionally healthy person is almost always ready to learn new skills.

Most people have many different arrows in their quiver of potential, but they usually wind up shooting only a few of them. There's a tremendous amount of wasted ability. It's a shame!

In our "better-be-the-best" society, all too many people avoid learning new things because they feel they won't succeed if they try to learn something. By not trying, however, they truly fail.

The joy of learning something simply cannot be measured by the excellence of the result.

Here are the kinds of statements I hear from people who are afraid of learning new things (all of the time).

"I once tried to paint something when I was in high school. It was awful. Art lessons would be a *waste* of time."

"I have a 'tin' ear. I could *never learn* anything in a course in music appreciation."

"I have three left feet. Sports are out of the question."

"It gets very cold some nights, and I don't want to bother to go to the creative-writing course. I'd just as soon watch TV."

Most of these people have no idea of how much they could, indeed, learn if they wouldn't insist on perfection for themselves. It's a shame that they will never try!

(NN's don't like to learn new things. They just like to do the same *old* thing over and over again—(so long as they get some admiration from others.)

Weed ——————→ Unless you can be the best in something, don't do it.

Seed ——————→ *Everything* we learn can enrich our lives.

❀

Teaching is a form of loving!

❀

What a good gift it is when *you* help those you love learn something new. It's perhaps one of the best investments in their future happiness.

Last Christmas, I knew a father who gave his fifteen-year-old son lessons in electronics. They bought components for a stereo-sound system, and together they are tinkering, soldering, and building.

A seventy-two-year-old woman, who grew up in France, offered to teach her newly married niece the old family recipe for bouillabaisse. By doing so, she transferred a skill that has helped her overcome many doubts about her ability to entertain friends and business associates.

Almost everyone has something that can be taught to someone else. Indeed, when you do impart a skill, you give a gift that doesn't wear out and doesn't break.

Sometimes, by giving the gift of a skill, you open a door to someone's future.

A dentist I know feels he owes his career to an old uncle of his who is now deceased. When this dentist was about twelve years old, his uncle, who had recently emigrated from Germany, found the boy sitting alone under a tree in an unhappy mood.

The uncle asked the boy what the trouble was, but it was clear that he was not, as yet, ready to share his thoughts with the man. The wise, older man decided that he would not be intrusive, and so instead of pressing the boy to discuss his problem in greater detail, he asked him if he knew how to whittle. The boy said he didn't but showed a spark of interest in learning. The uncle took out his pocketknife and selected a piece of wood for the boy. The two of them soon carved a rather humorous-looking dog.

As the months rolled by, the boy started to bring some pieces of wood to his uncle, and his uncle taught him increasingly sophisticated techniques of whittling. Soon the boy became extremely accomplished and began to carve intricate figures out of wood, stone, and soap.

When in college, a biology professor, impressed by the young man's ability—both in biology and with his hands—suggested to him that he would probably be a fine dentist! And he is!

Sometimes, people who are sensitive to the needs of someone they love, will give the gift of learning something new as an antidote to despair.

Larry B., age fifty-two, was becoming a bit—no quite—concerned about his wife, Marcie.

Now forty-nine, Marcie seemed to be losing her zest for living and her optimism. While their four sons were growing up, Marcie was always busy with one thing or another. She was the best den mother the town ever had, and she was always involved in parents' activities when the boys reached high school. Infuriated by some ridiculous educational policies, she ran for the school board and served for two consecutive terms.

Now that the four boys were all away at school, Marcie just didn't seem to be her old self.

It was hard for her to become enthusiastic about any project, and she constantly complained of fatigue and vague physical distress.

A comprehensive, physical examination at a well-equipped university clinic revealed no physical reasons for her continuing complaints, and her doctor suggested she was probably suffering from plain, old depression. She really missed all the activities that she had been involved with—and in her boredom was about to retreat into illness.

The doctor's diagnosis confirmed Larry's own hunch, and he decided on a possible cure.

Larry ran a rather successful and busy real-estate agency, and he told Marcie that he would like to "teach her" the real-estate business. At first, it took a lot of urging because Marcie had lost a lot of faith in her own ability. After a while, however, she did come into Larry's office and started to work along with him.

Larry then suggested she take a course to prepare her to take the exam for a real-estate license. She took the exam and passed.

All of that was two years ago. And now Marcie, in addition to being "better than new," is a highly successful real-estate broker. She hardly even knows when she gets a headache!

Larry's gift of teaching her something new was, indeed, just what the doctor ordered!

❦

I often teach a graduate course in psychology at William Paterson College in New Jersey. Most of the students who take the course are in their early or mid-twenties and were graduated from college within the past few years.

Mixed in with this younger group is usually a number of students who come back to graduate school after having raised their families. Some of these people are thinking about changing careers or starting a new career.

Almost always, these more mature students will meet with me at the beginning of the term and will express their anxiety about "getting back into the academic world." Some of them are almost apologetic about being there.

It's funny, but they usually wind up being my best students, and they almost always do better on the exams than anyone else.

They do well because they *want* to be there. They are *motivated* to learn.

Seed ─────────→ When we are strongly motivated to learn
something, we usually can do it.

(NN's don't like to work hard to learn something. They feel that knowledge should be given to them because they are so wonderful.)

❦

Yes, motivation is terribly important in learning something. As a matter of fact, psychologists know that unless you are strongly motivated to learn something, you'll learn very little—if, at all.

People simply do not learn if they are *passive* participants. They begin to learn when they *actively* want to know something.

Recently, a teenage girl I know got her driver's license. For years, she had visited her grandmother who lived in a small city about fifty miles away from her home. I guess she must have gone there at least a hundred times during her lifetime, but her parents always drove her back and forth.

A couple of weeks after getting her license, this girl was allowed to drive to her grandmother's house alone. The girl related to me her shock and dismay at losing her way several times during the trip.

"I must really be dumb," she complained. "I just didn't know which way to turn."

"You never *needed* to know how to get there before," I replied.

In my work with families, I know that many efforts that parents make to teach their children a skill fail because people forget about the important role that motivation plays in learning something new.

When you can increase someone's motivation to learn something, you often can help to focus and direct their efforts.

One girl of eight, for example, had a lot of musical ability. Her piano teacher felt, however, that she seemed to be losing her motivation to practice. She suggested that the girl might become more motivated if she had a goal that she could aim for.

Her parents, after some discussion, decided that it would be fun to arrange a small recital for their daughter, and in consultation with their daughter, picked a Sunday, three weeks away. A guest list of relatives and a few friends was compiled, and a new dress was bought for the occasion.

From that moment on, the child became increasingly enthusiastic about practicing, and the recital, I'm very happy to report, was a resounding success.

Weed ——————→ People learn things when they are exposed to them.

Seed ——————→ People will not learn *anything* unless there is motivation to learn.

❧

Perhaps the most important factor in helping people learn something is to understand the magic power of REWARD!

We simply can't learn if there is not a reward!

Most of the time, people make the mistake of thinking that

a reward, in order to be effective, has to be something very big or elaborate.

Big and elaborate rewards have their place, but most of the time *small* rewards are more than adequate in helping a learner learn.

One ten-year-old boy, for example, was being taught to ski by his father. His dad loved skiing, and he wanted his son to have as much pleasure with this sport as possible. In order to reward learning, the father told the boy that he would buy him his own set of ski equipment as soon as the boy could come down from the top of the intermediate slope without falling.

The boy practiced, and after a few days of skiing was able to navigate the hill quite well. His father was delighted, and he promptly kept his word and bought him a fine pair of skis, poles, and boots.

In talking with me about the situation, the boy confided, "I was sure glad to get those boots—but you know—I was even *happier* to know that I could get down that hill without breaking my neck!"

Yes, *mastery* of a new situation can be the *reward* that can reinforce the learning.

Why, it happens all the time.

—Charles K., age eighteen, is tinkering with his old junk of a car. He finally cleans the corroded cables from the battery, and the car begins to run. As a result of this *reward*, Charles wants to learn even more about cars.

—Sally R., age twenty-six, is preparing for a dinner party. She's having trouble getting her salad dressing to taste the way she would like it to. She adds a half a teaspoon of tarragon mustard, and she finds the taste that she was looking for. As a result of this reward, Sally wants to learn even more about cooking.

—Eric V., age six, is looking at a brand new book. There's a word in it that he never saw before. He tries to sound it out—tr–a–in. *Train*—that's it, thinks Eric. As a result of this *reward,* Eric wants to learn even more about reading.

Lots of things can serve as *rewards* for learning. Here are some of the things that psychologists have found to be effective as rewards:

1. stars on a chart
2. an increased allowance
3. a new toy
4. lunch at the local hamburger restaurant
5. satisfied curiosity.

In my own experience with people, however, I find that one of the most important rewards of all is plain, no-nonsense *attention* and *approval.*

Yes, in family situations I am always astounded to see how people will work as hard for attention and approval as they will for any larger reward.

It's important to remember this when you try to teach anyone you love anything at all. You always have to ask yourself, "What *reward* can I give?"

Seed —————⟶ Without reward, there is no learning.

Seed —————⟶ There are many different rewards, but sometimes attention and approval are better than anything else.

The planter of the carob tree would like approval and attention as rewards. These cost nothing, and they can be classified as being completely renewable resources.

❦

If you want to teach someone you love something new, here's something you have to know. You better learn it well, or you're not likely to get results.

Important Rule:

PUNISHMENT IS NOT THE OPPOSITE OF REWARD.

When you try to use punishment and threats to teach something, you're not likely to teach what you intended to teach. Sometimes, you teach someone to be resentful and angry. Sometimes, you teach them that they shouldn't try anymore, and so they give up.

Edward R., age twelve, had watched his father working in his vegetable garden every summer. Sometimes, Edward helped his dad, and that was also a source of gratification.

During the spring of the year that Edward was twelve, he hit upon a rather ambitious idea. He told his dad he would like to start his own vegetable garden that summer and that he wanted to set up a small stand in front of their home and sell the vegetables they raised.

Ed's dad was initially very enthusiastic about Ed's plans, and father and son spent lots of pleasant times planning the garden and ordering the seeds.

So far—so good!

Ed and his dad then staked out the area of the garden and

marked it with string. Ed asked if he could borrow his father's spade and hoe to turn over the ground.

Ed worked for a couple of days and then showed his father what he had done.

So far—so good.

"You didn't dig it deeply enough," said Ed's dad with some annoyance.

As Ed continued to work on his garden, he began to make a lot of the usual mistakes that beginning gardeners almost always make.

Ed's dad, instead of being patient with Ed's mistakes, showed his disapproval and took him to task for his errors. He thought that his criticism would be helpful! Without *reward* for his efforts, however, Ed gradually began to lose interest in the garden. The more he lost interest, the more his dad became critical.

One Saturday, Ed asked his dad if he could borrow the wheelbarrow so that he could remove some stones.

Ed borrowed the wheelbarrow, but a friend came by and Ed went off with his friend to play some ball. He forgot to put the wheelbarrow back in the shed. There was an overnight rainstorm, and the following morning Ed's dad was furious when he went outside and saw that his wheelbarrow was wet.

"You'll never use my tools again," he screamed at Ed.

And you know what? Ed *never* did. He learned to *hate* gardening. What a shame!

Weed ⟶ We teach best by being critical.

Seed ⟶ We are always on safer psychological ground when we use *reward* rather than *punishment*.

148

Seed ⟶ Mistakes are a vital part of learning something new. If you can't *stand* mistakes, don't *try* to teach anyone anything new.

Seed ⟶ When people try to learn something new, they often "bite off more than they can chew." It's a good idea to help them cut their *project* down to size without causing them to feel *they* are being cut down.

Any behavior you reward is likely to reoccur! That's crucial to remember!

Sometimes in my work with families, I'm astounded to see how people—because they don't think about what they are doing—reward someone else's undesirable behavior. Sometimes, with the best intentions, they even reward the very behavior they want to eliminate.

I was once consulted by a physician about his seven-year-old girl. He was concerned because she frequently complained about her health and would repeatedly go to the school nurse with complaints that she didn't feel well. The father was a busy man, and he was unable to spend as much time with his family as he would like. He was also turned off by his daughter's physical complaints since he heard so much of the same thing every day in his office.

I decided to see them as a family, and a couple of sessions were spent in getting to know them better.

During the third session, the secret of this girl's repeated physical complaints became exposed.

The mother and daughter arrived for the session at the regular time, but the father's nurse called to say that there was an emergency and he would be delayed.

Twenty minutes after the session began, the father rushed into the office, very rushed and harassed. He kissed his wife and then began to talk to me.

As soon as he did, his daughter said, "Daddy, my throat hurts. It really feels bad."

Automatically, the father took out a tongue depressor and his light. He looked at his daughter's throat and then gave her a kiss, "It's all right, kitten! Your throat is perfectly fine."

It was precisely this *attention,* given without awareness, that was gradually turning the child into a full-fledged hypochondriac.

When the father was instructed to put his daughter's health in the hands of a local pediatrician—and to give her more attention for other things besides her health—her repeated complaints about her health gradually became less frequent.

Seed ⟶ Often we are the ones that cause and help maintain other people's undesirable behaviors.

Seed ⟶ We have to be careful that we reward *desirable* behaviors.

Some of us aren't very good at teaching those we love! We become too impatient; we make too many demands; or we feel that our loved one isn't learning fast enough. When that happens, it's important to step back a bit and to remember that if they *knew* it, they wouldn't have to *learn* it!

I bet that even the carob-seed planter made some mistakes when he planted some of his seeds.

Some Additional Seeds

1. Pencils have erasers on them for a reason! A mistake can teach you what *not* to do.
2. You can't teach something to someone in an effective way if you're angry at him/her.
3. In order for people to learn something, they have to be *mature* enough to be able to do it.
4. Don't try to teach people anything if *they* don't seem to want to learn.
5. People learn best by doing.
6. *Encouragement* is the lubricant that can keep the learning machine going at full speed.
7. A skill that may seem very simple to you may be very difficult to someone else.
8. The more skills we have, the richer we are.

11. The Gift of Really Listening

It is the disease of not listening, the malady of not marking, that I am troubled withal.

—Shakespeare, *King Henry IV*

Do you know the story about the woman who returned from spending a year in the Peace Corps?

She came back home with her new husband, and as her parents watched her get off the plane, they were horrified to see that her husband was carrying a spear, a set of rattles, and a shield. He also wore a bone through his nose.

"No, you dummy," screamed her mother. "I told you to marry a *rich* doctor."

Yes, some people never listen carefully enough to get an accurate or a whole message!

Few of us know how to listen to others in an effective manner. What an important gift we give when we learn to listen, really listen, to those we love!

Often when someone tries to talk to us, we are in such a hurry to get our own message across, that we interrupt the person in the middle of the communication.

The famous English Prime Minister, Benjamin Disraeli, wisely commented, "Nature has given us two ears but only one mouth."

Indeed, in my work with people, I am convinced that a great many situations and problems between people could be resolved if people would spend twice the time in listening instead of *talking*. Really listening to others and what they are trying to say!

It's not always easy to listen to others when they talk. All too often, we interrupt someone in our own efforts to get *our* message across. We often begin to tell our tale before the other person has a chance to finish. However, when we restrain ourselves from saying anything until the other person is finished, the results can be very gratifying.

This past summer, my teenage daughter came home about a half-hour late. I was angry that she had violated what I considered to be a rather liberal curfew for a girl of her age. As she started to explain her lateness, I was about to reprimand her. I decided, however, to really listen to her explanation. When she had finished, I truly understood the predicament that she had found herself in when she tried to get a ride home at the right time. I said little but listened a lot. A few days later, she spontaneously kissed me and said, "Thanks for understanding what happened a couple of nights ago!"

There are a lot of jokes about people who go to a therapist, and the therapist doesn't say very much of anything. But anyone who tries to help people with their problems soon learns that people are helped much more quickly—when they are trying to work out a problem—by a helpful ear rather than a wagging tongue!

Good therapists know that people can usually work out their own problems if they have someone who will listen rather than have someone who will tell them what to do.

When we listen to people carefully—and resist our natural impulse to tell them what to do—they find their own solutions. And someone's *own* solutions are really the best ones.

Weed ——————————→ When people ask for our advice, we should give it to them immediately.

Seed ——————————→ It's best to help people find their *own* solutions to their problems rather than impose our own ideas on them.

❦

A couple of months ago, I was talking to a family. During the session, the teenage boy brought up a problem. He had been looking for a job, and had received two job offers. The first offer was for a job working as a busboy in a local restaurant. This job required him to work from 4:00 P.M. to midnight on Friday, Saturday, and Sunday. It paid well, but he wouldn't have much time to see his friends or attend any of the parties in town. The other job was in a supermarket and was from 3:00 P.M. to 8:00 P.M. every night. This job didn't pay as well as the first, but it would certainly permit him some more time to have a social life.

The boy had no sooner mentioned his dilemma when he was interrupted.

The conversation went like this:

Mother: "It's your senior year in high school. There will be a lot of parties, and *I* think you should leave some time for you to enjoy them. You *should* take the job in the supermarket."

Boy: "But I need a lot of money for college next year. If I take the job in the restaurant. . . ."

Father: "Of course, you *should* take the job in the restaurant. You need the time during the week to study."

Boy: "But I would like to see my friends. . . ."

Mother: "And you *should* see your friends. . . ."

Boy: "But I need the money. . . ."

Father: "And you *can* earn the money if you work in the restaurant."

Me: "Sounds like *you* have a *tough* decision to make."

Boy: "It sure is! You know, I guess it's best to wait to make a decision until I hear about that other job in the gas station tomorrow afternoon!"

It happens all the time! As soon as we let others know that *we understand* what they are saying—that we are *really listening*—they feel free to go on and tell more about themselves. They, then, usually grow and get stronger as they use their *own* good judgment.

❦

We become good listeners when we "reflect" back to others what they have been saying.

When a person hears us *reflect* a feeling, he or she knows that the message has been received and understood. Or, at least there is a chance to correct an error in our reception of the message sent to us.

That's what we call active listening.

Here are some examples of good *reflections* that demonstrate our attempts to listen and that serve to open channels of clogged communication.

A.—Arlene: "It's been a terrible, terrible day. The dog ran away, and the septic system backed up, and Pete is running a fever of 102 degrees."

Martin: "Wow, it seems as if everything went wrong."

B.—Stephen: "I lost the Johnson account, and the mechanic told me I need a whole new transmission put into the car."

Susan: "You had quite a day, didn't you!"

C.—Bruce: "My physics teacher gave us three chapters to read, and my English teacher told us the term paper is due next week. I also have a history quiz that I have to take tomorrow morning."

Mom: "You really feel overloaded, don't you?"

Here are some examples of the kind of comments that are likely to cut the wires of communication and tell the other person that you are *not* listening to them!

A.—Joan: "It's been a terrible day. The dog ran away, and the septic system backed up, and Pete is running a fever of 102 degrees."

Bill: "Well, what do you want me to do about it? I had a pretty terrible day myself."

B.—John: "I lost the Johnson account, and the mechanic told me I need a whole new transmission put into the car."

Rita: "You should have done what I told you."

C.—Son: "My physics teacher gave us three chapters to read, and my English teacher told us the term paper is due next week. I also have a history quiz that I have to take tomorrow morning."

Mom: "Well, you should prepare for these things in a more
serious way than you have been doing."

(NN's aren't interested in hearing what *other* people have
to say. They know it all—all the time!)

The fastest way to show you are not listening to what is
being said to you is to say either directly or indirectly that the
feelings being expressed are *wrong!*

Now, here's something important to know if you want to
learn how to give the gift of being a good listener.

FEELINGS ARE ALWAYS RIGHT!

Yes—always.

A feeling is *never* wrong! Because, after all, that's the way a
person feels. The *facts* that are producing the feeling may be
erroneous, but someone's feeling is *always* right!

Take worry, for example!

Perhaps, the most unthinking comment I so frequently hear
is, "Don't worry!" If the person who was worried had effective
techniques for controlling the worry, why, of course, he or she
wouldn't worry! But if people are worried, they are worried!

I once worked with a couple who had many problems. Not
least among the problems was the fact that the wife was a
chronic worrier. Her worries focused particularly on dying from
cancer at an early age. Often, when she was alone and frightened,
she would begin to worry about having cancer. When this would
happen, her husband would say (almost routinely), "Don't
worry! It's silly to worry! Your last physical examination showed
you were in perfect health, and I'm sure there's nothing wrong
with you."

157

Each time her husband said, "Don't worry," she felt more alone and more isolated than ever before.

There was, indeed, a *very* good reason why she worried about cancer. It was a way of punishing herself for angry feelings that she had but that she couldn't come to terms with in a direct fashion! It was only when her husband became sensitive enough to her needs to ask her questions such as,

1. "Why do you think you're worrying about cancer now?"

or

2. "You know, I noticed you began to worry again since Sunday afternoon. What's going on?"

that she started to come up with some meaningful answers!

If you want to give the gift of really listening, *never* tell people what they should feel. (NN's do it all the time!)

"What do you mean, you're afraid of the dark! No six-year-old, big boy of *mine* could be afraid of the dark."

"Isn't that silly—to say you don't like school. *Everyone* likes school! In *our* family, everyone has always loved school. Why, your cousin Eleanor was a schoolteacher a long time ago."

"You don't like baseball? Of course, you like baseball. All *boys* like baseball."

Weed ⟶ If you tell people that their worries are foolish, they will snap out of them.

Seed ⟶ It's foolish to tell people what to feel. People feel what they feel.

Deed ⟶ If you listen carefully to what people tell you—without telling them what to feel—their feelings might then begin to change.

158

❦

Do you know that someone's definition of a bore was a person who talked when *you* wanted him or her to listen?

When we develop the art of effective listening, people think we are great conversationalists! There are so many lonely, isolated people in this world who would welcome the opportunity to have *you* listen to them, even if it's just for a little while.

❦

A Psychological Study

One recent study compared the behaviors of happily married couples to the behaviors of couples who were unhappily married. It was found that in a happy marriage couples tended to communicate better and that they developed effective techniques of *listening* to each other.

Yes, listening to each other can help a lot.

One technique of listening effectively is to develop a variety of signals that let the other person know that you're listening and what your response to their message is. These signals are called feedback messages.

In their simplest form, feedback signals are simple listening noises.

Did you ever get a telephone call from a long-winded person who keeps talking to you? Did you realize that in order to show the person that you were still at the other end of the line, you started making listening noises such as,

"Mmm"

"Oh?"

"Ahh!"

These are primitive listening noises. But they are effective. If you want to see *how* effective they are, the next time you're talking to someone on the telephone, try not making any noises at all! I'll wager that within forty to fifty seconds, your caller will respond to your silence by saying something such as, "Are you there?" "Were we cut off?"

More sophisticated feedback signals tell the person that you're talking to someone about your response to the message they are sending.

Some of these feedback techniques would be things such as, "Yes! I hear what you're saying."

"Go on!"

"I get the first part of it. Tell me more about the part with Judy. . . ."

"I understand!"

When you give feedback you are, in effect, telling the sender of the message what impact the message has on you!

❧

If you would like to become a much better listener than ever before, here are three very helpful and very basic hints that might help you achieve that goal.

1. Don't Cut Off Someone Before You Hear Everything.
   This is a very common problem. Ern may be listening to Frances, and because Frances sometimes tends to become overinclusive, Ern tends to reach a conclusion before

Frances is finished telling him all the facts.

Sometimes the conversation goes like this:

Frances: "Hello Ern? Listen! I'm not feeling well. I. . . ."

Ern: "That's awful! Why don't you take a couple of aspirin? I'll talk to you later. . . ."

Frances: "How will that help my stomach virus? I guess he knows something I don't know."

2. Don't Play Judge

Len: "Elaine and I had a fight again tonight. . . ."

Joe: "I don't blame you for getting mad at her. She gets annoyed about anything. I think she hates all men. Listen, why don't you call me tomorrow?"

Len: "Maybe it wasn't such a good idea to sell the house without talking to Elaine about it some more."

3. Don't Give Advice So Freely

Carol: "I think that I've about had it with Carl. Tonight he came home and he. . . ."

Jill: "Get rid of him! You can get a better husband than Carl if you call up the want ads! I don't know why you keep hanging in there. At any rate, I have to hang up now. Bye."

Carol: "I guess any man could get mad if he found out that his wife withdrew everything from the savings account!"

Weed ⟶ I'll play it cool and silent. That will let them know that I'm listening.

Weed ⟶ I can figure out what she's saying before she even tells me. It's usually the same old problem.

Weed ⟶ I have a good ear for what's going on, and I can tell pretty quickly who's right.

Weed ⟶ If she would just listen to me, I could tell her how to fix it all up.

Seed ⟶ I can help a conversation by giving some good feedback.

❧

Do you know that if you really listen to people you can get a pretty good idea of what they are *going* to do?

Consider Suicide

Most suicide victims give clear warnings to those around them that they are planning to kill themselves.

Post-mortem studies of suicides have shown that the overwhelming majority broadcast their intent. Sometimes, however, we don't want to listen to their pathetic cries for help.

Eric N., for example, was terribly unhappy after his girlfriend left him for someone else.

"I can't take it anymore," he said to Bob. "If I continue to feel this way, I'm afraid I'll do something that would be terrible."

"Ever since she left me," he told Wanda, "I can't sleep, and I keep thinking that I want to die."

"I just can't get over the fact that she's really gone!" he told Fred. "I think I'm going to get into my car and crash into the highway divider."

—Bob thought that Eric was feeling sorry for himself.

—Wanda thought Eric was acting like a big baby.

—Fred thought Eric was asking for sympathy.

The next day, Eric was found dead in an auto crash. The police thought it was a peculiar accident, but some of his friends had other ideas about what happened.

Consider Runaway Wives

Do you know that more American wives than ever are simply disappearing? They just run away without a trace.

One woman, for example, was reported to have been riding along with her husband in their car when their windshield became icy. She told her husband to scrape the front windshield while she scraped the back window. And he saw her run away— and he never saw her again.

But most runaway wives, like

A. most runaway children,
B. most college dropouts,
C. most army personnel who go AWOL,

give sufficient warning. *If* (and it's a very big *if*) we would only try to listen!

When we listen to people, we listen not only to the things they say, but also to the things they do.

In recent years, psychologists have demonstrated that people broadcast their feelings not only by what they say but, more importantly, by the way they act.

That's what we call nonverbal communication. If we really want to listen to people, we learn to read their nonverbal communications, as well as the things that they actually tell us!

One psychologist, for example, has shown that when people

look at something that truly interests them, the size of their pupils actually increases.

Yes, your pupils get bigger when you look at something that has interest for you.

It's for this reason that clever medieval women used to put a substance in their eyes that would dilate their pupils. As the pupils became dilated, potential suitors (even though they didn't know exactly what cues they were responding to) listened to the message that these women were interested in them and tended to find the women more attractive.

To this day, we call this chemical substance belladonna (literally, beautiful woman), and if you go for an eye examination, the doctor might put a couple of drops into your eyes to see what's going on in there. (No, the doctor doesn't use those drops to make you look more beautiful.)

When we learn to listen to nonverbal messages, we can listen to things that we never heard before.

We start to learn that

1. a tapping foot can indicate boredom.
2. a clenched fist can signify unexpressed rage.
3. tightly pursed lips can mean that someone is closing off things wanting to be said. It may also mean disapproval.
4. arms clasped around oneself may mean that someone feels that he or she is in the need of comfort.

Another Psychological Study

Dr. Ernst Beir studied a group of fifty newlyweds who were between the ages of eighteen and twenty-four.

He asked each husband or wife to rate the degree of satisfaction with the marriage. Strange to say, even though these couples hadn't been married for a very long time, many of them were already experiencing marital problems.

He then videotaped sessions in which he jointly interviewed each couple. The videotapes were then reviewed by a group of judges who were trained to judge nonverbal cues to behavior.

They found that happier couples

1. showed more eye contact.
2. laughed more with each other.
3. touched each other more frequently.

Yes, if you begin to listen to nonverbal messages as well as verbal ones, you can learn an awful lot you never would have known before.

(NN's aren't interested in listening to what people have to say to them. They are interested only in what they have to say to people.)

Some Additional Seeds

1. Nonverbal messages become as important to us as verbal messages if we truly try to listen very carefully.
2. Do you know that nonverbal messages are the same from culture to culture. People in New Guinea, for example, are able to recognize emotions as portrayed in photographs, as well as people in Western culture?
3. A listening sound may be even more valuable in establishing communication as a talking sound.
4. Listening is usually more important than talking in understanding someone.
5. When most people talk, they aren't asking for answers. They will find their own answers if you just *listen* to them carefully.

6. Never—but never—attack someone's feeling about a situation.

7. When you learn to listen carefully to someone, you can reach heights of psychological awareness that you never thought were possible.

8. Do you know that when you really—I mean really—listen to someone, you are extending them a marvelous and valuable psychological gift!

12. The Gift of Fun

> There are men who suffer terrible distress and are unable to tell what they feel in their hearts and they go their way and suffer. But if they meet one with a laughing face, he can revive them with his joy. And to revive a man is no slight thing.

> —NAHMAN OF BRATZLOV, from *Joy of Jewish Humor*

DURING TIMES OF MALAISE and unhappiness, the gift of fun can, indeed, revive the sagging spirits of another human being.

NN's don't like to give fun to anyone else in their pursuit of their own needs. They wet-blanket the joy and happiness of everyone around them. They extinguish tiny sparks of fun and dampen the roaring fires of another person's enthusiasm.

Did you hear the recent joke about a classic example of wet-blanketing?

According to this story, Thomas Alva Edison was out in his laboratory one night, working feverishly on developing a filament that would glow when electricity would pass through it. He tried hundreds of substances. He tried the hair from an elephant's tail, but it didn't work. He tried a fiber from a palm frond, but that didn't work. He tried an iron wire, but it burned out too quickly.

At 3:00 o'clock one morning, exhausted by his labors, Edison tried a thin filament made of tungsten and, lo and behold, it lit up the entire laboratory. Edison knew he had hit upon an extremely important invention that would revolutionize the world.

In the midst of his joy and excitement, he bounded up to his bedroom, where his wife was sleeping. Clutched in his hand was his newly invented light bulb. He woke his wife to show her.

"What time is it, Tom?" she asked.

"It's three-thirty, darling," Edison replied.

"Then why don't you turn off the light and come to bed?"

You know, we *all* know people like that.

We all know people who destroy the happiness and joy of people around them by dwelling on the negative and dark sides of things. They can find the flaw in even the most perfect situation —and by doing so, can ruin fun for everyone else.

A few weeks ago, I heard a rather sad story about a surprise anniversary party.

A young woman I've been working with for some time has been suffering from painful bouts with mild, yet naggingly chronic, feelings of depression. She remembers that when she was a child her house was a rather gloomy place where there was very little time for fun or enjoyment. Everything was always serious and dour.

She remembered an incident which occurred when she was about seven years old that seemed to symbolize the prevailing mood of her home.

At breakfast, one morning, her older brothers told her a funny story and she began to laugh. Her mother, finishing her cup of coffee, admonished her, "You know what they say. If you laugh before seven, you'll cry before eleven."

Her sense of humor and joy, dispelled by such sobering thoughts, soon disappeared, and gradually, like her mother, she began to become overly serious and humorless.

During her marriage, her husband did all he could to revive her sagging spirits, but it wasn't until she was in therapy for some time that she started to make some real progress.

Feeling more alive and free, she decided it would be a lovely thing to give her parents a surprise dinner party for twenty friends.

My patient worked for many days to arrange the party for her parents. She carefully arranged the guest list, cleaned her house, and prepared a lovely meal.

The party was a great success, and all the guests seemed to have had a good time.

After the party was over, my patient's father thanked his daughter profusely for the wonderful party, and his eyes sparkled as he spoke about his pleasure.

Finally, her mother spoke. "You shouldn't have gone through all that trouble, dear. It was very nice of you to try. The roast beef was a little too well-done."

My patient burst into tears and ran upstairs.

In recent years, psychologists who have studied depression have come to learn that many depressed people are depressed because they find it difficult to permit themselves to have fun.

Even when they are given the gift of fun, they take it to the service counter and exchange it for a wet blanket or a grab bag of sad thoughts. In doing so, they become more unhappy and more depressed.

Weed ———————→ There's something wrong with fun. You can't live a serious life and have fun at the same time.

Seed ———————→ An attitude of being open to fun can be the antidote to feelings of depression and unhappiness.

If laughter is the best medicine, then early inoculation with a sense of fun, during one's childhood, can prevent many an unhappy malady later on in life.

We give children the gift of fun when we help them find joy in ordinary small events. We almost always have the choice of making a situation into a lesson in fun. A long car trip to visit family friends can lead to a nightmare of bickering for two young children in the back seat of the car with nothing to do.

Did you ever drive with two young children? If you did, I bet this sounds familiar.

Sally: "That's my side of the seat."
Joe: "No, that's my side of the seat."
Sally: "I want the window open. I get carsick."
Joe: "I want the window closed. I'm getting cold."
Sally: "Are we there yet?"
Joe: "Are we there yet?"
Sally: "Mommy, get Joe away from my side of the seat."
Joe: "Mommy, make Sally shut her window."

These are the times that try parents' souls!

Now, there are a few choices that you have in handling these tough situations.

Choice #1—"If you don't knock it off, Daddy will stop the car, and you'll both have sore rear ends."

Choice #2—"This is the last time we'll take you any place. Next year, Mommy and I will go to Disneyland by ourselves."

Choice #3—"I was speaking to your aunt last week, and she told me that your cousins always are nice and quiet when they take a trip. I don't know what's the matter with you."

Choice #4—"Let's see how many license plates from different states we can spot before we get to Minneapolis. I'll keep a list, and whoever spots the most will get a special dessert at dinner. There's one from Tennessee."

Choice #5—"Old MacDonald had a farm. Come on, I bet you know some other animals."

Yes, you have some choice in how you want to handle that rough situation. You can give a *gift* of fun—or you can make the situation worse.

By turning to fun, we can often save our very sanity, and, by doing so, insure our very survival.

In times of crisis, if we can fortify ourselves with humor, we can often soften a blow to our pride or to our self-esteem. Like a suit of armor, the capacity to laugh at ourselves, as well as at the absurdity of a situation, can serve to protect us.

Several years ago, I remember a rather poignant movie about the brutal Communist takeover in Czechoslovakia. There was a sense of terrible tragedy as people were forced out of their homes by the police and loaded into prison vans to be taken away to detention camps.

In one touching moment, an old man saw that his wife was about to break down as she was leaving her old apartment and her prized possessions. The man tried to soften the blow for his wife. "Hurry up, Maria!" he called. "Let's not miss this van. The best people in Czechoslovakia are already in jail, and I think we should get there before they start taking in just anybody."

Wise, courageous people know how to give the gift of fun to those they love!

Weed ——————→ A lot of situations are terrible, and anyone who sees the humorous side in them must not have any genuine feelings.

Seed ——————→ Most situations contain some element of humor in them.

Seed ——————→ If we can find a bit of fun in an already bad situation, we can sometimes prevent *bad* from becoming *worse*.

Seed ——————→ It's a wonderful thing to bring a smile to the face of someone we love.

❦

Do you know that an attitude of laughter and fun can heal. Yes—really heal!

Psychologists and physicians who have studied the psychological effects of laughter know that there are many positive physical changes that occur when we laugh. Our muscles relax, we take in extra oxygen, and there are many other physical effects as well.

Although the medicine of mirth is not completely understood, there are dramatic instances in which it works.

In a case history reported in detail in the *New England Journal of Medicine,* the noted editor, Norman Cousins, reported his recovery from a very severe disease from which his doctors gave him only 1 chance in 500 to recover.

In developing a battle plan to fight this illness, Cousins and his physician, Dr. William Hitzig, decided that among other experimental methods of treatment, they would try to mobilize the affirmative emotion of laughter in order to enhance a healthy response in his body's chemistry.

Do you know what Norman Cousins did?

He ordered a series of amusing movies sent to his hospital room. (He was particularly fond of "Candid Camera".)

As he watched some of his favorite reruns, Norman Cousins found that "ten minutes of genuine belly laughter had an anesthetic effect and would give me at least two hours of pain-free sleep."

Psychologists know that just as fun can help heal a wounded body, so, too, can fun and laughter help heal a wounded mind.

Humor, for example, is a very effective way of diffusing an anxiety-provoking situation.

One woman, for example, suffered from a very severe case of arthritis. She had tried all kinds of traditional remedies, but she couldn't seem to obtain very much relief. Finally, she decided she wanted to try acupuncture, and went for a series of treatments. When friends or relatives anxiously inquired about her progress, she would diffuse everyone's anxiety by saying, "Of course, acupuncture works. Did you ever see a sick porcupine?" As she and the people around her laughed, some of the tension was dispelled.

When we can laugh at ourselves and at our own situations, we can stop taking ourselves so seriously. If we can laugh, we can temporarily gain a sense of mastery over an otherwise very tough situation.

A few months ago I was consulted by a young couple who had been having increasing marital difficulties. It seemed clear that many of their problems had originated in a relationship in which their channels of communication to each other had become clogged with the silt of resentment and unexpressed feelings.

Mrs. C. was able to express her feelings of anger toward her husband in no uncertain terms. But Mr. C. could not confront angry feelings directly and, besides, he didn't feel he had any direct defense against his wife's rather sharp tongue.

After putting up with a lot of nagging and complaining, Mr. C. got back at his wife in a very indirect way. He took a girl from his office out for dinner, and afterward he spent a few hours at her apartment. They danced and talked, and then Mr. C. went home.

Naturally, the office grapevine leaked this incident to Mrs. C. and, as could be expected, she was in high dudgeon! Nevertheless, at her husband's urging, she agreed to visit a psychologist to see what could be done to save the marriage.

During the first session, Mrs. C. expressed her indignation. She wouldn't put up with that stuff! She wanted a divorce! She didn't deserve such treatment!

I tried for a while to suggest to her that perhaps it would be wise to try and understand what was going on in the marriage. Her husband pleaded with her to reconsider her decision to see a lawyer. She would have none of it.

When it became clear to me that I would only be falling further into her game of wounded pride by urging her to think about saving the marriage, I changed tack and said, "Well, I guess you have made up your mind! One robin may not make a spring, but in *this* case, one lark sure made for a fall!"

She began to smile, and her attitude began to soften. She realized how she was about to allow one incident to destroy an entire, complex, involved relationship. She agreed to try to work on her marriage.

And you know, they are slowly making good progress.

Seed ————————→ Humor can be the best antidote to false pride.

Seed ————————→ When we stop taking *ourselves* so seriously, we can begin to look at others in a more realistic way.

(NN's like to look at only themselves.)

Most people in America have already won the age-old battle with humanity's basic needs.

Most people now have

1. enough food
2. adequate shelter
3. a car that works (most of the time)
4. some warm clothes for winter and some cool clothes for summer.

Having won the basic-need battle, however, all too many people I know are in danger of losing the war against deadly dullness and beastly boredom!

175

Many years ago, the philosopher Nietzsche made the comment that "against boredom, even the gods themselves struggle in vain."

Most of our grandparents worked twelve to fifteen hours a day. When they weren't working at their jobs, they would be working at home. They were always working at one thing or another, and the very idea of *leisure* was a concept that, for the most part, was beyond their wildest dreams.

Today, there's an awful lot of people who don't know what to do with all of that newly found leisure. Some of them haven't even given themselves permission to *have* leisure, and when they do get some free time, they simply feel too guilty to enjoy it in a constructive way.

For many years now, psychologists have known about a condition called Sunday depression. People who have Sunday depressions usually feel fine so long as they are working. As soon as there's no work they have to do, they start feeling tense, depressed, and uncomfortable.

George A., age fifty-three, had a classic case of Sunday depression. During the week, when he was working as an accountant, he felt fine. On Sundays and holidays, however, he felt awful. When he went back to work on Monday mornings, he again started to feel better once again. His wife was becoming annoyed and impatient!

As George spoke about himself, the reasons for his Sunday depressions became clarified.

When he was a child, his parents owned a small newspaper and candy store. In order to make even a small profit, George's parents had to open the store at six in the morning and didn't close the store until nine at night. Whenever George saw them, they were working.

176

And so, George never learned how to play! After a time, George came to realize that his parents' circumstances were quite different from his own and that he needn't feel guilty if he had some free time.

I knew that he had come a long way when I learned that he had joined a hiking club. Now almost every Sunday (and some Saturdays as well), George permits himself to have the fun of exploring new trails.

Other people *misuse* their free time. They get involved in excessive TV-watching, drinking, meaningless and empty sexual encounters, or they work off excess energy by making mischief for themselves or others.

One man, for example, is semiretired and so has a good deal of free time on his hands. You know what his hobby is? He likes to sue people. That's right! He likes to *sue* people!

He collects injustices the way other people collect stamps. (He and everyone around him would be a lot better off if he did collect stamps instead of injustices.)

In pursuit of his hobby, he found

1. a can of tuna that didn't smell right, so he started a suit against the tuna company (and the supermarket where he bought it, too).
2. a loose sidewalk that wasn't repaired that caused him to trip, so he started a suit against the neighbor's insurance company.
3. a big stain on his suit when it came back from the dry cleaners, so he started a suit because of the suit.

Seed ⟶ It's great to have some leisure time, but it's even better to know how to use it in *constructive* ways.

❦

People have to *learn* how to use their leisure time constructively. It just doesn't happen automatically.

In school, a good teacher, in addition to teaching academic skills, also teaches children how to use their free time in constructive ways.

One marvelous teacher I know would encourage every child in her class to develop a variety of hobbies—and would help that child learn as much as possible about that hobby.

Indeed, I'm convinced that it's important to teach children how to balance *fun* and *work*.

All too often, in recent years, teachers have steered away from any *work* if it wasn't *fun*.

Work is fine!

Fun is fine!

Work doesn't always have to be fun!

It's important to find a good balance. Several years ago, Sir John Lubbock wrote in *The Pleasures of Life:* "The world would be better and brighter if our teachers would dwell on the Duty of Happiness as well as on the Happiness of Duty, for we ought to be as cheerful as we can, if only because to be happy ourselves is a most effective contribution to the happiness of others."

In the family, there are lots of ways of teaching healthy attitudes toward leisure time. I feel, for example, that children are short-changed if, by the time they become teenagers, the parents haven't

1. had them help bake some cookies on a day that the family was snowed in.

2. taught them how to read the different "mint" markings on pennies.
3. played Monopoly and landed on Boardwalk with two houses on it.
4. eaten peanut butter and jelly sandwiches in the woods.
5. caught a frog together.
6. played some kind of word game.

❧

A few years ago, I was in an airport in Florida. Most of the people there were families who were coming back from vacation.

An announcement was made that the plane had some engine problems and that the departure would be postponed for two hours. A loud moan arose from the passengers in the lounge.

A half hour later, I took a stroll around the lounge to see what people were doing. Here are some of the things I saw:

1. One father had borrowed a deck of cards from the airline and was teaching his children to play "Go Fish."
2. One mother was reading a book to her children.
3. One father was yelling at the kids that, "He'll never take them any place again."
4. One mother was loudly complaining about the delay to an airport attendant while her six-year-old daughter looked increasingly apprehensive.

What would *you* do in such a situation? I know that it's rough to have a plane delayed, but you *could*—yes! you could just use that time to give the gift of fun!

(I also saw an NN who was screaming at a pilot who was walking down the corridor, "How can you do this to me?")

❦

Play is children's work! It's through the medium of play that children learn about the world. It's by playing house that you start to understand how people respond to one another.

It's through the medium of play that children work out undischarged feelings of threats or fears. It's by giving an imaginary shot to a doll that you can take away some of the sting of last week's penicillin injection.

Children love and respond to adults who give them the occasional gift of playful fun.

Psychological Study

In a recent study, children were asked what they liked about grandparents. Very young children liked grandparents who gave them material things. By the time children were eight or nine, however, *getting things* was no longer important. These children preferred grandparents who became *mutually* involved in activities.

They preferred grandparents who gave the gift of fun!

By the time children are eight or nine years old, they would rather go *mutual* than *material*.

I once knew a grandfather, by the way, who had children from blocks around coming over to visit him. He always had a little joke, or a guessing game, or a little silly activity to offer them.

He must have taught hundreds of children how to find the little man's face inside the peanut! For those of you who missed out on meeting this man, I'll tell you what to do. The next time you open a fresh peanut, take the reddish skin off the nut carefully. Then very gently pull the two halves of the peanut apart. At the place where they were joined, there's a spot that acts like a hinge. If you look at it *carefully,* you can easily imagine a nose and a little round face. Once you have located it, try sharing that little piece of fun with a child you know.

Every time I think of this man, I imagine that peanuts must be first cousins to carob seeds!

Some Additional Seeds

1. All adults have a little bit of a "child" inside them.
2. When you choose to share a joke with someone, rather than a complaint, you give a very precious gift.
3. You can practice—yes practice—seeing the humorous part of almost any situation.
4. If you don't know what to do with children, there are some great suggestions at your local library.
5. Try making someone you love smile, and you'll feel good as well.
6. Turn off the television at dinner time and talk with the family. You'll be surprised at how much fun you can give them if you don't use dinner time as a time for criticism.
7. Have you done anything "silly" recently for a person you love?
8. Eric Sevareid once said, "Next to power without honor, the most dangerous thing in the world is power without humor."

13. The Gift of Letting Others Give to Us

For in truth, it is life that gives unto life—while you, who deem yourself a giver, are but a witness.

—KAHLIL GIBRAN, *The Prophet*

SEVERAL YEARS AGO, on a hot and rainy summer afternoon, my wife and I were entertaining some friends at our home. Suddenly, there was a tremendous crash, and a sheet of flame cut across the room. It took a few seconds to realize that our house had been struck by lightning. Fortunately, no one was hurt, although one wall of the house was damaged by the bolt. I could smell smoke and saw that some of the insulation was smoldering.

I went to the telephone to call the fire department. While I was on the phone, my three-year-old daughter, who had been amazingly calm throughout all of the ensuing commotion, asked my wife, "Why is Daddy calling the fire department?" "Because Daddy might need some help," my wife replied, "and the firefighters are people who are trained to *give* that help."

At that point, my daughter broke into sobs and came over to

hold me. "Why would anyone have to *give* help to Daddy?" she cried. "Daddy *gives* help to other people. Why would he need help?"

Several hours later, after all of the sparks were extinguished and a temporary patch placed on the charred wall, I explained to her that, in life, no one is on the *giving* end all the time. Sometimes, we need others who will *give* to us.

In my work with people, I am often astounded at the large number of people who have never learned that important lesson that my young daughter learned that scary afternoon.

In this very complex world in which we live, there are, indeed, many times when we *must* let *others* give to *us!*

Some people, isolated and superior, live in a tower of pride. They often are very comfortable when they can give to others. They cannot, however, tolerate a situation in which others give to them.

Because they falsely associate giving with inferiority versus superiority, some people simply will not let others give to them. Sometimes, such an attitude can be fatal not only to a human relationship but also to a human being as well.

Several years ago, I knew of a physician who was probably the most respected member of the medical community in the town in which he lived and practiced. Other doctors, if they encountered a particularly difficult case, would send their patient to this man for consultation.

One day, one of the other doctors in the hospital commented, with some circumspect hesitation, that he didn't look too well. The first doctor acknowledged that he hadn't been feeling well. The second doctor suggested that he would welcome the opportunity to be of whatever help he could be to the man. "Thank you for your interest," replied the first doctor in a rather brusque manner. "But *I'm* the senior man on this staff, and I can look after myself."

Several months later, he died of an illness which, if it had been treated in time, could have been cured.

So used to giving, this man could not accept the thought of taking.

After the funeral, his friend who had tried to talk with him, felt wretched and guilty. "Why didn't he let me help him?" he asked.

Do you know that there are a lot of needless deaths from heart attacks in this country every year? A lot of these deaths would not occur if patients would only ask others to give them some aid as soon as they have symptoms.

Some people, ashamed of having to take help from others, will hesitate calling the police or the ambulance squad until it's too late!

Weed —————————→ Independent people take care of everything themselves. It's shameful to get
help from others.

Seed —————————→ A healthy person knows there are times
when we have to let others give to us.

In every large city, there are some people who abuse welfare. These people cheat and take whatever they can get. We all know that.

But do you know that in every large city there are also many older people who are so ashamed of having to *take* welfare that they never apply for benefits they are entitled to? They can give, but they are unable to take even though they need and deserve the help.

❦

The joy that you feel when giving to others is felt by others when they give. Sometimes, persons who feel insecure *always* insist on being on the giving rather than the receiving end of every human transaction.

Two couples used to go out for dinner very frequently. They would enjoy these evenings a great deal, but often an otherwise pleasant evening would be spoiled when the check came. One of the husbands, wanting very much to be the nice guy, would always grab the check and pay for the dinner. The other couple gratefully accepted this gift of a good dinner on several occasions with sincere appreciation.

After a few more incidents of check-grabbing, however, one of the husbands told his wife that he did not want her to make any more dinner appointments with these friends. "If I can't pay my own way," he explained, "I just don't feel right about going. I don't mind him picking up the check sometimes, but I have to be allowed to take a turn also!"

Yes, when we let others give to us, and when we can accept their gifts in a generous and mature manner, we may be giving *them* one of the most important gifts of all!

Weed ─────────→ It's always better to give than to receive.

Seed ─────────→ Sometimes, it's kinder to receive than to give.

❦

When we let others give to us—and when we can take their gifts in a comfortable way—we sometimes are giving them the gift of a growing sense of *self-confidence*.

One man I know, for example, was about to convert his basement into a den. He planned to hire a carpenter who specialized in remodeling basements.

His seventeen-year-old son, who was rather handy with tools, pleaded with his father to be allowed to do the job.

"I can do it, Dad," he said. "If I run into any problems, I can always speak to the carpenter." The father, deciding to give his son a chance to give the family the gift of his work on finishing their basement, agreed that the boy could do the job, provided he would accept some advice from the carpenter.

The father spoke to the carpenter, who agreed to supervise the alteration of the basement, and every few days he came by to see how the boy was doing.

And you know what? He did just fine!

The completed basement was certainly not as well-finished as if the carpenter had done the work. Some of the nails were a bit crooked, and there were a few hammer marks on the paneling.

But, by allowing the boy to *give* him the "gift" of construction, the father had given the boy the even more important *gift* of the feeling of a job well-done.

❦

Once there was a mother of three children who broke her leg during a family ski vacation. When the family returned home, the doctor told the woman that her leg would have to remain in a cast for six weeks. Walking was restricted to the use of crutches and then only for a very few minutes each day.

The husband was about to hire a housekeeper, but their fifteen-year-old daughter objected.

"Let *me* take care of things," she said. "I can do it! I will be able to get dinner started when I get home from school, and if everyone else will pitch in, I'm sure I can do it."

Her parents agreed to let her try, and she did, indeed, do a fine job of both caring for the house and taking care of her mother.

In the process, she received the very precious gift of the feeling of being grown-up.

❦

One very sensitive, psychologically aware woman I know makes her ninety-year-old grandmother work for her. Yes—she puts that old lady to work every time she comes to visit.

Her grandmother lives in a senior citizen residence and is involved with many of the activities at this well-run facility. "The bad thing about this place, though," she confided to her granddaughter, "is that they do everything for you."

Two or three times a year, this grandmother would be taken out of the nursing home by her granddaughter. Once, during one of these visits to her granddaughter's home, she baked some cookies. As her great-grandchildren ate the cookies with relish, they asked her what life was like when she was a little girl in Sweden. Because of the interest shown, her step quickened and her face began to glow.

Taking her cue from her grandmother's reaction, the granddaughter now gives her a very special and individualized gift. Each time she comes to visit, the granddaughter has a comment such as, "Grandma, I'm so happy you're here. I have to have a very big luncheon next week, and the kids have cleared out all the cookies from the freezer. So you better get to work!"

As the old lady mixes flour and sugar and shapes the cookies into circles and stars, she feels very well, indeed, for she has been allowed to *give*. And she gets the gift of the feeling of being useful.

❦

One of the worst feelings of all is for a person to feel that he or she has nothing to give to anyone else. Yes! That's a terrible and painful feeling for someone to have.

Many psychological studies of middle-aged executives who lose their jobs show that the suicide rate of this group is high.

If a person has measured a sense of self-worth in terms of being able to give financially, he or she may become angry at losing a job and may choose to "execute" himself or herself for having become a surplus commodity in a tough job market.

At times, the only antidote for such a state is to create a situation where the unemployed person can once again feel that he or she can give something to someone else.

One fifty-five-year-old man, for example, lost his job. For a few weeks, he remained rather buoyant and did all the usual things. He wrote a resume, he went to some employment agencies, he called some of the contacts he knew.

After two months of fruitless searching, this man became more and more depressed. Soon, he had trouble sleeping, he lost weight, and he began to avoid talking to any of his old friends. His attorney-son, concerned about his father's emotional health, decided to run for the local school board. "You're going to be my campaign manager," said the son to his dad. "How can I be your campaign manager?" the father replied. "I don't even feel like getting out of bed in the morning!"

"I don't care how you feel," his son said, "I *need* your help. And that's that."

The father was, indeed, a little slow in getting started, but after a while he got into the swing of things. He

1. called some old friends and told them to vote for his boy.
2. tacked up lots of posters.
3. yelled at the editor of the local paper because his son was misquoted.
4. spoke to a great many people in town.

As a matter of fact, one of the people to whom he spoke knew of a job that was available.

His son lost the election, but because he gave his father the gift of letting him give, they both turned out to be winners.

Weed ⟶ Letting people do things for us is an imposition.

Seed ⟶ By letting people do something for *us,* we can often be giving *them* a very important gift.

Seed ⟶ Most people, if they feel they have nothing to give, begin to feel terrible.

We give the gift of letting others give to us when we let them know what we want. It's important to us to let others know what they can give if they choose to please us.

All too often, however, people feel that they want to be polite and accommodating, so they don't provide the information that someone else may need to give us a gift.

Consider

Situation #1—He: "What would you like for dinner, sweetheart?"

She: "Anything at all will be fine."

Situation #2—He: "What would you like for your birthday?"

She: "Anything at all will be fine."

It's much better to say things such as,

1. "I feel that a steak would be good."
2. "For my birthday, I could use a nice pair of earrings."
3. "Would you please hand me the soap so I can wash the baby?"
4. "I could use some help in carrying the laundry upstairs."
5. "I would appreciate some help in raking up the leaves."
6. "That's a beautiful picture that you drew of the seashore. Could I frame it and hang it in my office?"

❧

Do you know that sometimes we need to give others the opportunity to give so that they can atone for some of the things they have done wrong?

Most people, as they go through life, do some things that they are proud of—and some things that they are a little ashamed of. Healthy people have a conscience that tries to put things right again by making restitution after they have done something wrong.

Psychological Study #1

One group of college subjects were led to think that they had harmed another subject in the study. After this experiment, these subjects were much more likely to donate a pint of their blood to the Red Cross than the group of subjects who did not feel they had hurt anyone else.

Psychological Study #2

Another group of college students were made to think they were giving other subjects in the study a painful electric shock. After the experiment, these subjects were much more likely to join a make-believe group that wanted to "Save California Redwood Trees."

When others have done something wrong, we give them an important gift if we will then accept a gift from them.

A simple *apology* is the best example.

If someone has wronged us and is willing to apologize, it's a gift when we accept the gift of an apology.

Sometimes, it's a good gift to allow someone to make restitution for having done something wrong.

For example, a man who loved dogs was driving along one day when a dog broke free from its leash and ran under the wheel of his car.

Although he was clearly not at fault, this man felt bad that his car was the instrument that caused a severe leg injury to the dog. As he stood in the street trying to tend the wounded animal, one of the children and the mother of the family that owned the dog came out to see what had happened.

The child began to cry, and the woman was about to berate the man for injuring her pet when she saw the pain in his eyes.

The man offered to drive the dog and the mother to the veterinarian. She accepted his offer, and the dog's leg was rapidly put into a cast.

"It was a bad experience," the man said when he told me about it, "but I'm glad that she let me help!"

Yes! When someone else feels guilty about something, we give a gift of kindness when we let the person make some restitution to us.

Seed ──────────→ Do you know that when children act as if they are "asking for it," they often feel guilty? It's good to find out what they feel they have done wrong.

Seed ──────────→ Accepting the gift of someone else's apology can lessen the burden of guilt for the other person.

❧

People often feel great when they know that they have given a gift of importance to someone else.

In one recent study of kidney donors, for example, it was found that, almost invariably, the experience of donating a kidney to someone else left the donor feeling much happier than before. "I feel I'm a better person, much happier than before. I've done something with my life," was a typical comment.

It is, indeed, a gift to be able to give—and people who work with other people know that they begin to grow as they stretch and reach out to help others.

Alcoholics Anonymous, which has helped so many people give up drinking, knows that a certain part of one's own rehabilitation—helping someone else stay sober—can help sustain one's own sobriety.

One woman I worked with hadn't had a drink for ten years. But she was about to! Her daughter had moved out of the country, and her husband had died—all within a period of six weeks.

She felt that she was about to go on a binge when she got a call from another member of her AA chapter. She spent several hours helping her friend, and when she found that she was able, indeed, to be of real assistance, she lost her desire to drink. "I guess there are still a few people around I can help," she said.

But do you know who most needs the gift of being able to *give*?

If you guess the NN's, you're right on target!

Underneath all the selfish behavior, there is a lonely, scared person who finds it so hard to *give* because of never having *received*.

1. Instead of having been given *time,* they were given things.
2. Instead of having been given a *good example,* they were shown indifference.
3. Instead of having been given *acceptance,* they were given criticism.
4. Instead of having been given the gift of being able to *see the best in people,* they were taught to find the worst.
5. Instead of having been given the *gift of privacy,* they were never given respect for their individuality.
6. Instead of having been given the *gift of self-esteem,* they were taught self-hatred.
7. Instead of having been shown how to *give up some bad habits,* they were taught more of them.

8. Instead of having been given the *gift of self-disclosure,* they were given crooked communication.
9. Instead of having been *helped to learn something new,* they were allowed to wallow around in old habits.
10. Instead of having been *listened to,* they were ignored.
11. Instead of having been given *fun,* they were given sadness.

No wonder so many of the NN's are unhappy. But there's a chance for them yet!

If we could help the Narcissist give to others, he could learn how much joy there is in being human.

The NN's could, indeed, grow. And when they do, they'll find out that it's even more fun to love others than it is to love themselves.

Why, they might even start planting some carob seeds for generations to come. That would be good for them. That would be good for you. That would be good for everyone.

And wouldn't *that* be good?